VIOLENCE
IN
URBAN AMERICA

Mobilizing a Response

Summary of a Conference

Committee on Law and Justice
Commission on Behavioral and Social Sciences and Education
National Research Council

and

The John F. Kennedy School of Government
Harvard University

NATIONAL ACADEMY PRESS
Washington, D.C. 1994

; report was approved by the Governing Board
ers are drawn from the councils of the National
of Engineering, and the Institute of Medicine. The members of the committee responsible for the report were chosen for their special competences and with regard for appropriate balance.

This report has been reviewed by a group other than the authors according to procedures approved by a Report Review Committee consisting of members of the National Academy of Sciences, the National Academy of Engineering, and the Institute of Medicine.

The National Academy of Sciences is a private, nonprofit, self-perpetuating society of distinguished scholars engaged in scientific and engineering research, dedicated to the further-ance of science and technology and to their use for the general welfare. Upon the authority of the charter granted to it by the Congress in 1863, the Academy has a mandate that requires it to advise the federal government on scientific and technical matters. Dr. Bruce M. Alberts is president of the National Academy of Sciences.

The National Academy of Engineering was established in 1964, under the charter of the National Academy of Sciences, as a parallel organization of outstanding engineers. It is autonomous in its administration and in the selection of its members, sharing with the National Academy of Sciences the responsibility for advising the federal government. The National Academy of Engineering also sponsors engineering programs aimed at meeting national needs, encourages education and research, and recognizes the superior achievements of engineers. Dr. Robert M. White is president of the National Academy of Engineering.

The Institute of Medicine was established in 1970 by the National Academy of Sciences to secure the services of eminent members of appropriate professions in the examination of policy matters pertaining to the health of the public. The Institute acts under the responsibility given to the National Academy of Sciences by its congressional charter to be an adviser to the federal government and, upon its own initiative, to identify issues of medical care, research, and education. Dr. Kenneth I. Shine is president of the Institute of Medicine.

The National Research Council was organized by the National Academy of Sciences in 1916 to associate the broad community of science and technology with the Academy's pur-poses of furthering knowledge and advising the federal government. Functioning in accor-dance with general policies determined by the Academy, the Council has become the principal operating agency of both the National Academy of Sciences and the National Academy of Engineering in providing services to the government, the public, and the scientific and engi-neering communities. The Council is administered jointly by both Academies and the Institute of Medicine. Dr. Bruce Alberts and Dr. Robert M. White are chairman and vice chairman, respectively, of the National Research Council.

This project was sponsored by the Centers for Disease Control and Prevention of the U.S. Department of Health and Human Services and the Harry Frank Guggenheim Foundation. Support for the case study in Appendix A was provided by the National Institute of Justice of the U.S. Department of Justice.

Library of Congress Catalog Card No. 94-65431
International Standard Book Number 0-309-05039-1

Additional copies of this report are available from:
National Academy Press, 2101 Constitution Avenue N.W., Washington, D.C. 20418

B312
Printed in the United States of America

CONFERENCE PARTICIPANTS

L. ANNETTE ABRAMS, Department of Sociology, Michigan State University

MICHAEL BEAVER, Director of Public Safety, Indianapolis, IN

GORDON L. BERLIN, Manpower Demonstration Research Corporation, New York, NY

SHAY BILCHIK, Associate Deputy Attorney General, U.S. Department of Justice

JOHN A. CARVER, Chief, Pretrial Services Agency, Washington, DC

MICHELE CAVATAIO, Office of the Deputy Secretary, U.S. Department of Education

MICHAEL CHERTOFF, U.S. Attorney, Newark, NJ

PHILIP J. COOK, Terry Sanford Institute of Public Policy, Duke University

SYLVESTER DAUGHTRY, Chief, Police Department, Greensboro, NC

BEVERLY WATTS DAVIS, Executive Director, San Antonio Fighting Back, San Antonio, TX

ROSS DECK, Senior Policy Analyst, Office of National Drug Control Policy, Executive Office of the President

PETER EDELMAN, Counselor, Office of the Secretary, U.S. Department of Health and Human Services

JULIE FAGAN, Director, Drug-Free Neighborhoods Division, Public and Indian Housing, U.S. Department of Housing and Urban Development

JAMES FOREMAN, Coordinator, Metro Orange Hat Coalition, Washington, DC

LUCY FRIEDMAN, Victim Services, New York, NY

RICHARD W. FRIEDMAN, Director, Juvenile Justice Advisory Council, Baltimore, MD

WILLIAM E. GLADSTONE, Special Advisor, Office of Senator Bob Graham

STEPHEN GOLDSMITH, Mayor, Indianapolis, IN

RALPH E. GRIFFITH, Director, Risk Management and Security, Prince William County Schools, Manassas, VA

WILLIAM GRINKER, Fellow, Twentieth Century Fund, Brooklyn, NY

NANCY GUERRA, Department of Psychology, University of Illinois at Chicago

DEBORAH HAACK, Colorado Department of Health, Denver

JOHN HAGAN, Faculty of Law, University of Toronto, Canada

JOEL F. HANDLER, School of Law, University of California, Los Angeles

FRANCIS X. HARTMANN, Executive Director, Program in Criminal Justice Policy and Management and Malcolm Wiener Center for Social Policy, Kennedy School of Government, Harvard University

PHILIP HEYMANN, Deputy Attorney General, U.S. Department of Justice

HOPE HILL, Professor, Psychology Department, Howard University

HAL HOLZMAN, Research Analyst, Office of Policy Development and Research, U.S. Department of Housing and Urban Development

MICHAEL B. JANIS, General Deputy Assistant Secretary for Public and Indian Housing, U.S. Department of Housing and Urban Development

SUZAN JOHNSON COOK, Domestic Policy Office, Executive Office of the President

PAUL JUAREZ, Department of Family Medicine, Charles Drew Medical Center, Los Angeles, CA

JANET JUBAN, Texans' War on Drugs, Houston

ED JURITH, Director of Legislative Affairs, Office of National Drug Control Policy, Executive Office of the President

JILL E. KORBIN, Associate Professor, Department of Anthropology, Case Western Reserve University

MADELEINE KUNIN, Deputy Secretary, U.S. Department of Education

JOYCE A. LADNER, Vice President, Academic Affairs, Howard University

LINDA LANTIERI, Coordinator, Resolving Conflict Creatively Program, New York, NY

GEORGE LATIMER, Director, Office of Special Actions, U.S. Department of Housing and Urban Development

ROBERTA K. LEE, Professor, Community Health, School of Nursing, University of Texas Medical Branch, Galveston

E.O. McALLISTER, Executive Director, Dade County Public Schools Police, Miami, FL

ELIZABETH McCANN, Manager of Public Safety, Denver, CO

JOAN McCORD, Department of Criminal Justice, Temple University, Philadelphia

JAMES MERCY, Chief of Epidemiology, National Center for Injury Prevention and Control, Centers for Disease Control and Prevention, Atlanta, GA

WILLIAM MODZELESKI, Director, Drugs, Planning, and Outreach Staff, U.S. Department of Education

MARK H. MOORE (*Chair*), Kennedy School of Government, Harvard University

GENE MORRISON, Office of Special Actions, U.S. Department of Housing and Urban Development

GEORGE NAPPER, JR., Commissioner, Children and Youth Services, Atlanta, GA

RICHARD NEAL, Commissioner of Police, City of Philadelphia, PA

MARY NELSON, President, Bethel New Life, Inc., Chicago, IL

JOHN NORQUIST, Mayor, Milwaukee, WI

JUDGE THOMAS K. PETERSON, Circuit Court Juvenile Division, Miami, FL

ALBERT J. REISS, JR., Department of Sociology, Yale University

EDWARD G. RENDELL, Mayor, Philadelphia, PA

WILLIAM RITTER, District Attorney, Denver, CO

LAURIE ROBINSON, Associate Deputy Attorney General and Acting Assistant Attorney General for the Office of Justice Programs, U.S. Department of Justice

DOMINGO RODRIGUEZ, Vice President, Chicanos por la Causa, Phoenix, AZ

JEFFREY A. ROTH, Abt Associates, Bethesda, MD

ARMANDO RUIZ, Executive Director, South Mountain YMCA, Phoenix, AZ

ROBERT J. SAMPSON, Department of Sociology, University of Chicago

ELLEN SCHALL, Robert Wagner Graduate School of Public Service, New York University

KURT L. SCHMOKE, Mayor, Baltimore, MD

MICHAEL SCHRUNK, District Attorney, Portland, OR

STUART SIMS, State's Attorney, Baltimore, MD

LAURA SKAFF, Assistant Commissioner, Social Services Administration, Minnesota Department of Human Services, St. Paul

MICHAEL SMITH, President, Vera Institute of Justice, Inc., New York, NY

DAVID STEVENSON, Office of the Under Secretary, U.S. Department of Education

MIKE STIERS, Division Chief, Investigative Services, Aurora Police Department, CO

DONALD SYKES, Director, Office of Community Services, U.S. Department of Health and Human Services

MARTY TAPSCOTT, Chief, Police Department, Richmond, VA

PAUL TAUER, Mayor, Aurora, CO

JOYCE N. THOMAS, President, Center for Child Protection and Family Support, Washington, DC

NANCY THOMPSON, Governor's Office, Lincoln, NE

STEVE THOMPSON, State Senator, Atlanta, GA

CHRISTY VISHER, Science Advisor to the Director, National Institute of Justice, U.S. Department of Justice

LOUIE L. WAINWRIGHT, President and Chief Executive Officer, Wainwright Judicial Services, Tallahassee, FL

JOEL WALLMAN, Harry Frank Guggenheim Foundation, New York, NY

DENNIS WEST, Director, Public Housing Authority, Portland, OR

DOTTIE WHAM, State Senator, Denver, CO

CATHY SPATZ WIDOM, Director, Hindelang Criminal Justice Research Center, State University of New York, Albany

WILLIAM WIIST, Houston Department of Health and Human Services, TX

Contents

Preface

The violence now occurring within our cities is a national scourge. The fact that minority youth are disproportionately its victims makes it a tragedy and a disgrace as well. For mayors seeking to establish civil, secure communities, no problem seems more urgent.

Yet, what to do remains uncertain.

The problem is not necessarily in the "science base" that society can draw on in searching for plausibly effective interventions. There are plenty of theories about the causes of violence, and no small number of facts useful in testing those theories. (For a complete survey, see *Understanding and Preventing Violence*.) And every day science is making progress in clarifying the theories and testing them against empirical evidence.

The problem, instead, lies in converting hypotheses about potential causes of violence into operational programs that have some prospect of success in reducing one or more aspects of the violence problem and that could be adopted and effectively implemented by hard-pressed communities and governmental organizations. In short, the problem lies in the domain of "action science" rather than "basic science."

To help deal more effectively with violence as it happens in today's cities and to accelerate the growth of the "action science" underlying violence prevention efforts, the National Research Council and the Kennedy School of Government teamed up to organize a special kind of conference. The conference design was based on several different principles.

First, we focused attention on what should be done rather than what was known. To do this, we gave people a case study to consider in which the problem of violence in a particular city, along with its first moves to begin solving it, were laid out.

Second, we looked at the problem from the vantage point of a particular governmental actor—a mayor. That was based more on a judgment about where the problem lies than what was the most effective level at which to take action. We remained open to the idea that to deal with the problem effectively, action might be required at other levels of government.

Third, we sought to combine the knowledge and experience of academics and practitioners; community activists as well as government officials; officials from the federal as well as local governments; officials from many different functional areas of government, ranging from maternal and child health to prosecutors and correctional administrators.

The ultimate aim of the conference was not only to advance the learning of the people who attended, but also to create a record of the thoughts, ideas, and proposals that emerged. How well we succeeded in this effort, we leave to the reader to judge.

What success we did achieve in both stimulating and organizing practical thought about how best to deal with violence in the cities owes a great deal to the organizers and participants. We owe a particular debt to four sets of individuals whose contributions made the greatest difference. First is the mayors, who gave generously of their valuable time both in advising on the structure of the conference and as key participants. Both as leading representatives of their communities and, we believe, as thoughtful innovators, they brought unique perspectives to the conference: Stephen Goldsmith, Indianapolis, Indiana; John Norquist, Milwaukee, Wisconsin; Edward G. Rendell, Philadelphia, Pennsylvania; Kurt L. Schmoke, Baltimore, Maryland; and Paul Tauer, Aurora, Colorado.

The second group are the rapporteurs, who were instrumental in shaping the conference and working as partners with the mayors in the management of the five task forces: Philip J. Cook, Duke University; Francis X. Hartmann, Harvard University; Michael Smith, Vera Institute of Justice, Inc.; Cathy Spatz Widom, State University of New York, Albany; and Jeffrey A. Roth, Abt Associates Inc. Third, we are indebted to the federal agency officials who advised on the structure of the conference and were invaluable as participants; their names are found in the list of participants. And fourth, the event and this publication would not have been possible without the efforts of the staff of the National Research Council's Commission on Behavioral and Social Sciences and Education: Susanne A. Stoiber, director, Jeffrey A. Roth, consultant, and Nancy A. Crowell, research associate, of the Division on Social and Economic Studies; and Eugenia Grohman, associate director for reports.

Finally, we are also extremely grateful to the foundations and government agencies that supported this activity: the Harry Frank Guggenheim Foundation and the Centers for Disease Control and Prevention of the U.S. Department of Health and Human Services sponsored and funded the conference, and the National Institute of Justice of the U.S. Department of Justice sponsored the case study discussed in this report and reprinted in Appendix A.

Mark Moore, *Chair*
Conference on Urban Violence

VIOLENCE
IN
URBAN AMERICA

Mobilizing a Response

1

Introduction

Americans increasingly perceive their communities to be menaced by violence and fear that public institutions cannot maintain social order. Violence—and the fear of violence—have changed the way people live, their interactions with intimates and strangers, the way they raise their children, and their confidence in public officials.

Across the country, states and cities debate strategies to prevent crime and punish criminals. A candidate's perceived ability to ensure law and order is frequently the decisive factor in elections. Congress is considering a range of legislation to combat crime and violence. The President has placed the issue of violence high on the national agenda, calling for a comprehensive public- and private-sector response. Despite this broad national consensus that things must change, however, there is little agreement about how to achieve change.

Within the last year, the National Research Council has published three major reports that describe what is known about various aspects of violent behaviors. The first, *Understanding and Preventing Violence*, provides a comprehensive synthesis of the research literature on violent human behavior and patterns of violence in American society. The second, *Losing Generations: Adolescents in High Risk Settings*, describes the environments in which today's adolescents are growing up, and the influence of context on the development of anti-social or self-destructive behaviors. The third report, *Understanding Child Abuse and Neglect*, analyzes what is known about child abuse and neglect, including its impact on adolescent and adult behaviors. Collectively, these reports, and a forthcoming volume from the Harry Frank Guggenheim Foundation, offer a wealth of research-based knowledge about the causes and consequences of violent behaviors and describe comprehensive research agendas to further scientific knowledge about the various manifestations of violence and the effectiveness of interventions.

In the normal course of events, the knowledge contained in these reports would work its way into the domain of practice over a period of years. Recognizing the urgent national need to formulate more effective strategies and interventions against violence—particularly in urban areas—the National Research Council in partnership with the John F. Kennedy School of Government undertook an experiment to try and shorten the process of translating research-based knowledge into program interventions for immediate use. The format was the Conference on Urban Violence, bringing together leading scholars of violence with citizens and public officials engaged in efforts to confront it.

In his remarks opening the October 7-9, 1993, conference, Bruce Alberts, chair of the National Research Council, urged participants to use the research knowledge contained in the reports in combination with the experience and wisdom gained from practice to suggest new approaches and interventions against the various manifestations of violence. He emphasized the importance and value of efforts to translate science into action and the role that practice-based knowledge can play in facilitating that translation.

In order to provide a way for participants to focus on potential strategies and interventions rather than a restatement of the problem, the conference was organized as a problem-solving exercise, using a case study approach developed at the Kennedy School. The case study for the conference was a fictional urban area, "Cornet City," of roughly 1 million people that had just experienced a weekend of violence—six unrelated homicides (see Appendix A). The participants were sent the case study prior to their arrival at the conference with instructions that they would be asked to develop realistic steps that could be taken by the mayor and other leaders of Cornet City in response to the overall increase of violence in the city.

The Cornet City murders varied in their characteristics and included an abused toddler, a convenience store clerk, a participant in a bar fight, a disgruntled employee, an estranged spouse, and an unexplained killing possibly connected with the sale of drugs. The clustering of so many killings in a 48-hour period, and a highly critical news report about the week-end carnage, provoked a political firestorm in the city. Officials were deluged with calls from citizens demanding action. In the words of one official of the (fictional) city: "The people who have been calling my office are just fed up. This violence is getting totally out of control, and they want something done about it. . . We have got to get these people off our streets."

In response to the public outcry, the Cornet City mayor appoints a task force that includes public health and safety officials, a local judge, the directors of social service agencies, public affairs, the police, city school officials, and representatives from other city departments. The mayor charges his "Antiviolence Task Force" to come up with a plan to deal with the violence facing the city and to present that plan to him within 100 days. Members of the task force are provided with briefings and other resources to familiarize themselves with patterns of violence in the city and with the resources available to the mayor.

Participants in the National Research Council/Kennedy School of Government conference were divided into five task forces, each led by an urban mayor: Kurt L. Schmoke of Baltimore, Maryland; Stephen Goldsmith of Indianapolis, Indiana; Paul Tauer of Aurora, Colorado; John Norquist of Milwaukee, Wisconsin; and Edward G. Rendell of Philadelphia, Pennsylvania. Each task force was asked to act as if it were the task force appointed by the mayor of Cornet City and to develop a feasible and plausibly effective response to violence in Cornet City.

Two briefings provided conference participants with additional information. First, key participants of the four recent academic studies noted above reviewed knowledge about violence and related urban conditions summarized the conclusions of their projects highlighting implications of the report findings for the Cornet City exercise (see Appendix B). Second, representatives of five federal agencies—the U.S. Departments of Education, Health and Human Services, Housing and Urban Development, and Justice, and the Office of National Drug Control Policy—summarized their departments' evolving plans to reduce violence as a background against which the mayor's group could formulate local plans involving federal resources.

Armed with this information, each conference task force deliberated and developed a set of recommendations to guide the mayor of Cornet City. The reports were presented and discussed at the conference's closing plenary session, which also included a discussion about the federal role in preventing local violence. The primary contributors at the plenary session were the federal agency representatives and the mayors, who drew on experiences in their home communities, as well as the discussions in the task forces.

This report summarizes the conference discussions. It should not be construed as containing findings endorsed by either the National Research Council or the Kennedy School of Government. No effort was made to craft participants' disparate views into statements that achieved both internal consistency and unanimous agreement. In addition, the limitations inherent in a short conference format prevented a disciplined evaluation of the ideas presented and the development of priority rankings. With these caveats, however, the ideas contained in the report deserve attention in suggesting effective roles for federal, state, and local governments and, most importantly, recognizing the critical role that must be played by families and communities. Conference participants produced:

- wide agreement on the assumptions and general objectives that should guide strategic responses to urban violence at the neighborhood, city, state, and federal levels;
- specific objectives and tactics to be pursued in urban violence reduction and recommendations to the Mayor of Cornet City on tactics for achieving them; and
- ideas about organizational innovations to increase the effectiveness of local governments in supporting community-based responses and federal efforts in supporting local responses.

The report follows the organization described above. Part 2 discusses the assumptions and general objectives that the participants suggested as a strategic plan for developing responses to violence in Cornet City. Part 3 expands those views into short-, medium-, and long-term objectives and suggests tactics that task force members thought might be effective in attaining them. Part 4 explores organizational issues that must be considered in establishing objectives and designing tactics. The appendices contain the case study and book summaries that served as background materials for the conference.

Although the five task forces all worked from the same case material and all were composed with the same mix of expertise, each was free to approach the problem on its own terms. Not surprisingly, each task force maintained its own view of the problem and mapped an individual course of action. Issues considered to be primary in one task force were deemed less important in others. However, as the report reflects, there was a surprising degree of convergence around major objectives and many tactics. In addition to the areas of broad agreement, the report adds ideas that were raised in one or more groups and were greeted with enthusiastic response when presented at the final plenary session.

2

Assumptions and Objectives

Just as each of the five task forces approached their charge in an individually distinct manner, in real life cities will approach the problems of violence very differently. Despite these variations, all of the task forces either explicitly or implicitly based their recommendations on four assumptions.

1.   Reducing violence is a national priority not only because violence injures and kills, but also because it imposes other high costs on American society.

As documented in *Understanding and Preventing Violence*, violent injuries and deaths impose huge costs on society: an estimated $54,000 per rape, $19,000 per robbery, and $16,500 per assault, including such costs as loss of life, pain and suffering, emergency and long-term medical treatment and rehabilitation, and psychological treatment of victims' posttraumatic stress. Other recent estimates place the total national cost of violence at more than $450 billion a year, including both direct costs and such indirect costs as the loss of economic activity in high-crime areas. Fear and other consequences of violence also damage society in many ways. For example, violence in homes, on streets, and in schools produces psychological trauma and fear that impede the social and educational development of children.

Other consequences of violence not only raise its social costs, but also contribute to an escalating cycle that increases future levels of violence. If frightened citizens remain locked in their homes instead of enjoying public spaces, there is a loss of public and community life, as well as of "social capital"—the family and neighborhood channels that transmit positive social values from one generation to the next. As violence becomes associated with particular neighborhoods, people and businesses move away, reducing property values and removing role models and economic opportunities. And as people in particular racial, ethnic, or socioeconomic categories are stereotyped as violence-prone, they are systematically excluded from the social networks that lead to legitimate economic opportunities. This exclusion further deepens social divisions and weakens commitments to traditional social institutions. Some members of the excluded groups then become involved in high-violence, illegal markets.

2.   Responding effectively to violence requires recognizing and also responding to the anger, fear, and despair it produces.

Conversations about violence in Cornet City suggested that anger and fear are aggravated when violence goes "out of control" by crossing some widely accepted social limit, for example, by killing an unprecedented number of victims in a short time, touching an unusually young or innocent victim, or violating a school, convent, tourist attraction or other place that had been considered safe. If, over time, responsible authorities appear impotent in responding to out-of-control violence, fear and anger may give way to more pervasive despair that "nothing can be done."

Controlling violence effectively requires defusing or redirecting those emotions of despair and impotence; otherwise, community residents may contribute to the actual violence problem and limit effective responses. Fearful residents may not cooperate with police, may remain immobilized in abusive home situations, or may acquire guns that are stolen and transported into criminal hands. Despair over violence discourages community efforts to reclaim public spaces and financial investments that might expand economic opportunities in neighborhoods that need them. Public anger sometimes precludes reasoned public debate over proposed violence control strategies that, politicians fear, will be scorned as "not tough enough." In the extreme, anger and despair may provoke violent vigilantism. Properly understood and channeled, however, citizens' anger over violence can be a welcome resource to beleaguered officials seeking to cope in their communities.

3.   Violence control initiatives must be as varied as the contexts from which violence arises, and they must exploit the strengths and address the needs that citizens recognize in their own communities and families.

Conference participants donated their time because of their concern over the nation's violence problem. However, it soon became clear that their cities were actually experiencing different violence problems than those in Cornet City, and than each other's cities, that those problems require different responses, that the afflicted neighborhoods have different resources for mounting those responses, and that community leaders have quite different philosophies about ethically permissible responses. This diversity suggests the futility of any attempt to design a "one-size-fits-all" national response to local violence. Indeed, participants recounted strong shared experiences of federally devised solutions that do more harm than good when implemented at the local level. Instead, what participants wanted from the federal government in the short term was improved management of federal law enforcement programs and information about a portfolio of promising interventions that might be tried at the local level. The time-honored plea for delivery of financial and other assistance that maintains accountability without sacrificing local flexibility was voiced by virtually all participants. In the longer term, participants wanted federal actions to address underlying problems in the economy and society that foster the conditions in which violence thrives.

The diversity of violence was illustrated in several ways. For example, youth violence in Phoenix and other western cities emerges from traditional gangs—highly organized, along ethnic lines, and concerned with turf protection; in contrast, youth violence in Washington, D.C., erupts around loose, temporary groups that lack the organizational discipline to negotiate truces. In some cities, murder rates soar during crack epidemics; in other cities, they fall during epidemics. And sadly, while police-community cooperation in the real-life model for the Southwood neighborhood of Cornet City eradicated "home-grown" violence surrounding a local drug market, it could not prevent the murder of the neighborhood convenience store proprietor by "outsiders"—a gang that specialized in robbing Korean-owned shops throughout the entire city. These examples underscore the need to remember that violence erupting from different causes will need different responses.

The conference also illustrated the diversity of community resources for responding to violence. For example, members of a Community Development Corporation (CDC) in Chicago reclaimed some public "turf" by setting up lemonade stands next to open-air drug markets. A Phoenix CDC led by former gang members provides varied social services such as residential drug treatment, school-based preventive drug education, shelters for battered women and their children, a recreation and therapy center for gang members, and congregate housing for the elderly. A coalition in Washington, D.C.—largely the creation of one committed man—has launched more than 260 neighborhood groups that follow a safe but effective patrolling model for drying up local drug markets. Two cities represented at the

conference had legacies of successful interagency problem-solving to prevent deaths—from fires in Milwaukee and from drug overdoses in Washington, D.C. And when local leaders of Operation Weed and Seed in Richmond, Virginia, came to fear a cutoff of federal support, they organized a
private-public nonprofit corporation to continue and expand the program.
While every neighborhood plagued by violence has some resources—human, organizational, or financial—plans for successful responses to violence must consider and respect the specific resources available in each
particular place.

Finally, discussions about Cornet City revealed important differences in
values that seem likely to arise in planning responses to violence in real
cities. One source of difference was the "triage question": whether resources should be allocated primarily or even exclusively to the neighborhoods in greatest need, reserved for high-need neighborhoods that retained
enough social and human capital to use the resources effectively, or used
for pilot projects in both troubled and strong neighborhoods. The discussions touched on accountability and efficiency, on the morality of "writing
off" any neighborhood, and on the practical value to troubled neighborhoods of having strong, politically "well-connected" allies to demand the
continuation of successful pilot projects after attention to violence wanes
and new demands on resources arise. Other differences arose over resources for criminal justice agencies. No one argued against a fair and
effective criminal justice response to violence, but several task forces had
vigorous discussions over the priority that such responses should receive.
(This issue is discussed more fully in Part 4.)

Another basic difference concerned the ages at which costly interventions with children should occur. Evaluations suggest that interventions
work more effectively with younger children (under 10) than with older
ones (teenagers). This knowledge provoked uneasy searches for fiscally
and ethically defensible paths between writing off part of a generation of
teenagers and young adults and "wasting" scarce resources that might be
more effectively applied to prevention during preschool and early childhood
years.

No attempt was made to resolve differences and create consensus on
these and other value-laden questions. Yet one consensus did emerge: that
genuine local differences in values, capacities, and needs make local planning of responses to urban violence a substantive necessity, not just a rhe-
torical claim. The dilemma for federal planners then becomes how to facilitate such planning without giving up necessary accountability.

**4.   Because there are few antiviolence interventions that have proven
consistently effective in reducing violence, prudent public officials must
respond to violence more like medical researchers following promising**

leads in a search for a cure than like physicians confidently prescribing a proven therapy.

A widespread public perception that local violence is out of control is a call to abandon "business as usual." Governmental accountability demands that public officials respond to the public's anger and fear: inaction leads not only to the risk of being voted out of office, but also, more importantly, to aggravating the violence-promoting effects of the perception that violence is out of control. Unfortunately, conference discussions made clear that social science currently offers only limited guidance about effective responses. Rigorous evaluations have found many plausible interventions to be ineffective or effective only under certain conditions. They have certified very few as effective according to the standard of "scientific certainty" (customarily, a statistical test of 95 percent confidence). And careful social scientists are likely to caution that even a "proven" intervention may not work in a different ethnic, socioeconomic, or cultural setting from the one in which it was tested. However, the urgency of a city's violence problem may create opportunities for innovative public officials to strengthen government institutions, to strengthen partnerships between public and private institutions, and to collaborate with social scientists in the search for more effective solutions.

The need for action under uncertainty is not unusual for public officials. But the discussions raised several themes about strategy development that seem especially important in the context of urban violence. First, violence will not be prevented or reduced without political risk. For example, some plausible and popular governmental programs or approaches do not work, but the political cost of not using them is high. In addition, news reports may distort some actions into reinforcements of negative stereotypes, thereby damaging nascent leadership in communities and feeding "us versus them" hostility played out on racial, ethnic, age, or geographic lines.

Second, grass roots participation in development of responses to violence is essential. Participation not only helps to "sell" a particualr action to the public, it also brings to the effort far greater community resources than the government has by itself. In particular, community anger over violence can be mobilized in helping to apprehend criminals, in changing a community's culture, in taking back public spaces from perpetrators of violence, and in sharing child-rearing responsibilities.

Third, a political leader who effectively communicates the urgency of responding to violence and the important roles community residents can and must play may be able to use a local violence crisis to achieve broad improvements in city services. A well-managed crisis can be a catalyst for making public agencies more effective and responsive, for strengthening families and social institutions, and for creating public-private partnerships.

Fourth, when public officials understand the uses of program evaluation and collaborate with social scientists, it is possible to respond to calls for action while building the knowledge needed to make future antiviolence programs more effective.

With the implicit or explicit foundation of these four assumptions, the task forces considered ways to carry them out. Their discussions resulted in a general conclusion and a set of objectives.

A plausibly effective response to violence requires a mix of immediate, short-term, and long-term efforts to achieve seven objectives:

(1) promote a more effective criminal justice response to violence;

(2) mobilize neighborhoods to cooperate with police in violence prevention;

(3) reduce violence hazards in communities;

(4) strengthen supports for children and their families;

(5) reduce violence in the home, which is both a problem in itself and contributes to violence on the streets;

(6) rebuild human and financial capital in communities weakened by violence; and

(7) promote a prosocial, less violent vulture.

As noted above, the conference was not intended to produce consensus about responses to urban violence. Nevertheless, the tactics recommended by the five task forces clustered around these seven objectives, and they form the structure in Part 3 for presenting the task forces' recommendations.

3

Tactics

This part organizes the task force recommendations to the mayor of Cornet City around the seven objectives that concluded Part 2. In each category, the objectives are ordered roughly by time, reflecting whether they are likely to produce immediate results, require months, or depend on long-term investments. Part 4 turns to innovations in local government organization and intergovernmental relations that the task forces believed would be useful in supporting the tactics described in this part.

Two words of caution. First, there is no scientific certainty about how to reduce violence, and few of the tactics recommended here have passed the test of scientific evaluations. Therefore, these tactics should be considered as options in portfolios of plausibly effective responses to urban violence. As with financial investments, these tactics carry no guarantee and require performance monitoring and evaluation; indeed, evaluating these tactics and revising them in light of experience is perhaps the best way to develop a national strategy to control violence.

Second, like any portfolio, the response to urban violence demands balance. Different task forces at the conference gave more or less weight to different objectives. However, none believed that achieving any single objective would be sufficient to produce meaningful reductions in violence. Perhaps the most often repeated statement at the conference was along the following lines: "The ideas we have on the table sound useful and important to me. But we're kidding ourselves if we don't recognize that we also have to maintain the criminal justice response, create economic hope for these kids and support the families that are trying to raise good kids, . . ."

With these cautions in mind, we believe that a balanced portfolio of tactics suggested to the mayor of Cornet City warrants serious consideration by actual jurisdictions in which violence seems somehow out of control. Many of the suggestions flow directly from insights provided by social science research reported in the National Research Council and Guggenheim studies. The suggestions reported here all survived the "face validity" test of being seriously considered and not discarded by a skeptical task force of senior scholars and policy makers concerned with urban violence.

Objective 1:   Promote a more effective criminal justice response to violence.

A more effective criminal justice response to Cornet City's recent siege of violence was widely seen as essential. The task forces offered four kinds of recommendations: improving emergency response, overcoming community fear of cooperating with criminal justice agencies, expanding options for intermediate sanctions and postincarceration aftercare, and making traditional criminal justice responses more effective. Although not explicitly stated, an underlying assumption supporting these tactics is that the police will be honest, and will treat members of the community with respect.

Improving Emergency Response

The Cornet City case opens with a futile attempt to report a shooting on the 911 emergency line. Jammed emergency lines are common in cities throughout the country. One task force called for "whatever it takes" to eliminate busy signals and recorded announcements on 911 emergency lines. Failure to immediately connect a 911 line was said to communicate in the clearest possible way that the police department, too, finds violence out of control. Clearing jammed emergency lines was a first-order priority for Cornet City because the inability of citizens to even call out for help has powerful symbolic as well as practical implications. In other cities or communities the key symbolism will be different. Whatever it is, the issue must be identified and swiftly acted upon.

To improve emergency response in Cornet City, conferees suggested (1) more 911 operators; (2) a "triage" system for handling incoming calls, although such systems need fine-tuning to avoid exacerbating poor police-community relations; and (3) public education campaigns to encourage reporting nonemergency events to a nonemergency line.

In the eyes of the task forces, the minutes and hours following the police response to a violent emergency offer several underexploited opportunities to solve the immediate crime, prevent new ones, and reduce community fear and despair. They recommended that the mayor:

• give enraged young relatives and acquaintances of murder victims immediate attention—from police, counselors, and the community—commensurate with their dual status as sources of help in solving the immediate case and potential violent perpetrators in revenge killings;
• keep the police officer on the neighborhood community beat informed regarding all 911 calls for assistance and the police response—to develop his or her own understanding of the community and to communicate as much as is feasible to satisfy residents' legitimate needs for information and reassurance;
• create an active Victim Assistance Unit that, while providing psychological and practical help to surviving victims and families, also advances the larger goals of reducing fear, promoting positive attitudes toward the criminal justice system, and creating channels for information that may be useful in solving the case; and
• mount immediate and visible police patrols in the vicinity of a "violence wave"—to reduce fear and encourage a helpful community presence on the street, even if patrols are not expected to advance the ongoing investigation.

Overcoming Fear of Cooperation with Criminal Justice Authorities

Community reluctance to cooperate with criminal justice authorities lessens the ability of the system to reduce violence by punishing offenders. Nationally, only about one-half of all serious violent crimes are reported to police, and witness reluctance is a significant and growing impediment to successful prosecution after arrest. Between 1974 and 1990, the percentage of felony cases dismissed due to witness problems approximately doubled for violent crimes and grew 12-fold for drug and other "vice" crimes in Cornet City. A judge there has called witness intimidation *the* major problem facing the local criminal justice system.

Conference participants saw effective, nonintrusive witness protection as both a right and a tool for reducing violence. As television crime shows describe incessantly, typical witness protection programs are designed for long-time racketeers with few family or community ties, who feel trapped between organizational death sentences if they cooperate and long prison sentences if they refuse to do so. Understandably, witnesses facing this dilemma willingly take extreme and disruptive measures to protect themselves. But for most witnesses who are law-abiding citizens, if they are faced with a choice between entering such a program and remaining silent, they are likely to choose silence.

Examples of tactics for effective witness protection can be found at all stages of the police and court processes, from investigation through pretrial release and prosecution. Specifically, task force participants mentioned the following:

- During house-to-house interviews, investigators should make sure they are not seen stopping at the homes of productive witnesses longer than ar other houses. Arrangements should be made for later, unobserved communication with these witnesses.
- For promising but hesitant witnesses, detectives should leave business cards with a request to "Call any time if you think of anything else." If suspicions of police corruption are widespread, the cards can direct calls to a nondepartmental telephone number or to the cellular unit of the community police officer.
- Investigators can minimize the need for courtroom testimony by developing independent corroboration from less visible witnesses or other sources.
- For high-risk times in cases for which witnesses have had to play key visible roles—such as immediately after a suspect's release before trial or following an acquittal—witness protection programs should incorporate useful principles from battered women's shelters, with their emphasis on temporary housing, psychological support, and minimal disruption to routine activities.

Expanding Intermediate Sanctions and Postincarceration Aftercare

The limitations of some juvenile and criminal justice system standard approaches, including incarceration, as tools for reducing violence, were raised in the briefings on National Research Council reports and in task force discussions. *Understanding and Preventing Violence* reported that while average prison time served per serious violent crime nearly tripled between 1975 and 1989, the level of those crimes merely oscillated, so that their number in 1989 was almost exactly the same as in 1975—about 2.9 million. Apparently, imprisoned violent offenders were replaced by new offenders on the street.

Losing Generations pointed to trends in the sanctioning of nonviolent youthful offenders that may help explain this replacement effect. Court decisions and changes in practice since the 1960s have brought increasing numbers of young people, especially minorities, into adversarial juvenile or criminal justice proceedings that place them at risk of incarceration for nonviolent and status offenses (such as curfew violations). Harsh punishments for minor offenses may set the stage for future violent offenses by compromising the youth's future prospects for legitimate employment. The mechanisms involved include the creation of court records that prejudice employers. Furthermore, prison isolation from job markets makes inmates' existing job skills outdated, and prison life itself appears to solidify social networks that perpetuate violence associated with ethnic conflicts and illegal markets.

Recognizing these problems, three task forces called for systems of intermediate sanctions intended to impose real punishment on adult and juvenile offenders, including the mechanisms and resources needed to enforce the sanctions while avoiding the costs and violence-promoting effects of imprisonment. The task forces urged that intermediate sanction systems include the following components:

• emphasis on community restitution, both to remind the offender that he or she is part of a community and to offset the community costs of crime and punishment with some return to the community;
• conditions that discourage further criminal activity, such as frequent monitoring so that a tightening or amending of conditions can follow immediately upon relapse and to ensure that offenders avoid certain areas, associates and activities;
• requirements and supports to help the offender begin to overcome personal barriers to economic success by participating in treatment for addiction to alcohol or other drugs, high school equivalency or other education, training in vocational and social skills, or special programs to overcome cognitive or ommunications problems;
• recognition that where laws provide for parole or other forms of postrelease supervision, intermediate sanctions can be used either as *alternatives* to incarceration for minor crimes or as postrelease *adjuncts* after release from incarceration for serious violent offenses.

Administering intermediate sanctions that address communities' priorities and individual offenders' needs requires less emphasis on cases and more on improving the quality of neighborhood life, restoring victims and communities, and diverting offenders' life courses from criminal to productive directions. In making these recommendations, the task forces recognized that the courts are not organized to ensure compliance with intermediate sanctions. Fines and restitution go unpaid, community service is not done. It is an important challenge for Cornet City and real cities to find or create the organizational capacity to implement this strategy.

With that major caveat in mind, task force members offered suggestions about how to construct a system of intermediate sanctions. One is sentences that reflect both the risk that offenders pose to the community and individual offenders' incentives, capacities, and needs (with safeguards against arbitrary or discriminating judgments). Finding the right sanctions requires a sophisticated risk analysis and motivational assessment. Monitoring the system requires periodic consultations between prosecutors and residents of all neighborhoods in a jurisdiction, to provide prosecutors with a clearer picture of neighborhood concerns and to inform residents about how prosecutorial decisions are reached. Enforcement of intermediate sanctions can be improved by stationing satellite probation offices in neighborhoods, where they can discover and respond to violations more quickly, recognize emerging neighborhood problems that may pose special risks to their clients' success, find and mobilize community resources, and exchange information with community police officers that should improve the effectiveness of both.

Making Traditional Responses More Effective

The innovations discussed above would represent new directions for most local criminal justice agencies in responding to violent crimes. In addition, the task forces discussed five ideas for making traditional criminal justice responses to violent crimes more effective without departing sharply from existing practice: extending court hours into the evening to reduce police overtime and detention costs; increasing the number of police officers; broadening access to juvenile court records; sentencing nonviolent offenders to military-style "boot camp" programs; and targeting gang leaders for arrest and incarceration.

Extending court hours was the only noncontroversial recommendation. However, all of the five struck some conference participants as reasonable ways to increase criminal justice system effectiveness at least marginally, without sacrificing due process. Discussions of the other four illustrate the need for local flexibility and participation in fashioning antiviolence programs that reflect local operating conditions and attitudes toward the criminal justice system.

Two kinds of opposition arose to the last four ideas. The first kind reflected operational concerns: Could such new practices or resources be managed effectively? The second kind revealed a certain lack of trust that a more efficient criminal justice response, even guided by principles of due process, would meet the needs of the minority neighborhoods most afflicted by violence. Losing Generations explains this lack of trust in terms of three factors: first, a historical legacy from times when the criminal justice system was used rather explicitly to "keep blacks in line;" second, uncertainty over whether local criminal justice systems would use new resources to reduce violence in minority neighborhoods or contain it there, away from predominantly white neighborhoods; and, third, perceptions of the juvenile and criminal justice systems as perpetuating a process that, perhaps inadvertently, mortgages the future employment and other life prospects of minority youth for the sake of crime reduction today. These questions, related to management and community trust, arose repeatedly in discussions of all but the first idea for improving the effectiveness of the criminal justice response to violence.

Extending Court Hours   The abolishment of night courts in most jurisdictions requires that police officers who work nights come in on overtime during the day for the arraignment of individuals arrested after court hours. This is an expensive use of unnecessary police overtime and an inefficient deployment of a scarce resource—community police officers.

Increasing the Number of Police Officers   Placing additional officers on the streets occupies a central place in current federal thinking and legislation. Therefore, it seems worth noting that none of the mayors or mock task forces expressed the view that more officers, by itself, would be valuable in Cornet City or their home cities. Nearly all participants, however, placed high priority on mobilizing neighborhoods to cooperate with police in planning and carrying out violence prevention.

As explained under Objective 2 (below), community- and problem-oriented policing are two approaches to accomplishing such mobilization, and they both place great demands on officers' time. Therefore, a federal initiative that combines resources for new officers with incentives and technical assistance for adopting these approaches will advance what the conferees identified as a priority. Because new officers and preventive policing both require training and integration, linking the initiatives may reduce the associated costs through consolidation. Some training and personnel costs might be avoided by following the Seattle, Washington, practice of using civilians rather than sworn officers in some community policing functions.

Broadening Access to Juvenile Records   Discussions of broadening criminal justice system access to juvenile court records also illustrated differences that seem best resolved at the local level. Several task force members believed that eliminating one of the remaining barriers between the juvenile and criminal justice systems, separate record repositories, was appropriate because of the violent nature of crimes now being committed by juveniles. Others believed that combining the repositories would exacerbate the adverse effects of both justice systems on minority youths' long-term employment prospects.

The primary issue is access to records by prosecutors shortly after arrest, when priority decisions are being made regarding charges, bail, etc. Following conviction, juvenile records are normally available to criminal court judges in presentencing reports. A 1986 recommendation of the National Research Council's Panel on Research on Criminal Careers may offer a starting point for resolving debates on this issue: to maintain separate repositories, to allow prosecutors temporary access to an individual's juvenile record following an adult arrest for use only in the instant case, but to transfer the juvenile record to the adult repository following any adult conviction. One useful variant might be to restrict the domain to cases involving violent crimes.

Creating Boot Camps   The discussion of boot camps also pointed up the need to encourage local flexibility. Boot camps, especially for youthful offenders, are gaining advocates in many states. However, conference participants expressed the view that boot camps alone result in neither lower recidivism rates than traditional punishments nor lower costs per inmate than prisons. In addition, some states that introduced boot camps for nonviolent offenders were surprised to experience *increases* in regular prison populations. This apparently occurred because of "net-widening": some nonviolent offenders who previously would have avoided prison wound up there solely because they failed the boot camp program. Legislation in at least one state that attempted to avoid the net-widening pitfall apparently erred in the opposite direction by excessive "net tightening": their new boot camps were drastically underpopulated because so few offenders met the stringent statutory eligibility criteria.

To achieve the desired outcomes, sentences to boot camps must be followed by concentrated efforts to ensure employment and shelter. No institutional corrections program is likely to have an enduring effect without an aftercare program. This is especially true with respect to boot camps, which produce high levels of motivation and energy. If these are not constructively channeled following release, the result is likely to be a more effective, rather than a reformed, offender.

Nothing in the discussion suggested that boot camps are necessarily a bad idea. However, the discussion highlighted the need to allow latitude for innovations to reduce recidivism or costs per inmate and for fine tuning to avoid the costly pitfalls of net-widening or net-tightening, and most importantly, to produce a a well-crafted follow-up program.

Targeting Gang Leaders   Some task force members called for priority—in policing, prosecution, and sentences to imprisonment—for gang leaders. Again, however, the discussion revealed the need to allow for local variation.

Gangs are thought to be an important source of violence in some cities, although not in others. Although imprisoning gang leaders may hamper their recruitment of new members, it may fail to interdict violent gang activity. Some participants reported success in reorienting the organizational skills of gang leaders rather than removing those skills from the community. For example, a successful 25-year-old community service and violence prevention organization represented at the conference was organized by former gang leaders and continues to draw young people out of gangs and into constructive community service. Finally, some participants expressed concern about the "networking" opportunities offered by prisons as gang leaders extend their spheres of influence by negotiating interlocking agreements with other gangs. "If you put enough of these guys in prison, you've got an executive retreat," explained one participant.

Objective 2: Mobilize neighborhoods to cooperate with police in violence prevention.

All five task forces urged that public recognition of the violence crisis in Cornet City and in real cities nationwide serve as a signal to begin a sustained process of building or rebuilding the will and the institutions needed for cooperation among community residents, law enforcement, juvenile and criminal justice, and other public agencies. This will require both the fostering of community-based institutions and a sustained effort by the criminal justice system—and by the police in particular—to build relationships of trust and confidence. Habits of distrust and fear built up over generations will not be easily or quickly overcome. Yet without community confidence in the integrity of the police and criminal justice systems, the barriers of silence that protect criminal elements within the community will not be overcome.

Specifically, participants recommended the following initiatives: a series of community meetings between police and residents; police-community collaboration in identifying "hot spots" for violence, diagnosing the underlying problems, and solving those problems; police assistance to the community in reclaiming public spaces from people who create social disorder and violence; and the establishment of permanent community policing programs.

Initiating Community Meetings

All the task forces recommended that whenever violence is declared "out of control" in some neighborhood, the *initial* police response should include an open meeting for neighborhood residents with police department representatives at all levels, from the chief to the neighborhood patrol officers. Although the agenda and tone of the first meeting will vary from one community to another, conference participants' experience suggest that the first meeting should usually accomplish a few standard objectives:

- Give residents a chance to "vent" about such matters as police inability to protect them, overly aggressive police responses, or suspected police corruption—even when the concerns may appear inconsistent with one another.

• Let residents know that police empathize with community frustration, recognize a shared responsibility for accomplishing shared priorities, and need the community's help.

• Begin developing a broad agenda of community problems to be solved together.

• Identify at least two measurable, quickly achievable tasks, one to be accomplished by the community and one by the police.

• Communicate a sense of continuity by introducing the chief's personal representative for follow-up contact and by setting the date and time of the next meeting.

Two kinds of objectives that may surface at the initial community meeting are to clean up a hot spot for violence or to reclaim a public space for public use.

Finding and Fixing Violence Hot Spots

One task force advised Cornet City's mayor to issue the following order to the police chief:

> Within two weeks, produce a list of locations in Cornet City where the patterns and concentration of police calls, ambulance responses, community perceptions, and other indicators suggest high risk of violence occurring. Prepare plans for addressing the underlying problems at those locations, whether they be the most dangerous bars, the most virulent open-air drug markets, or particular addresses, telephone locations, intersections, or cash teller machines where the distinguishing features are less apparent. Plans to correct the 20 top hot spots of this kind are to be drawn up with, and implemented with, neighboring residents, merchants, schools, churches, and the rest of the community where that is possible. And we expect it to be possible more often than not.

This recommendation drew on criminologists' and epidemiologists' findings in several cities that a handful of places often accounts for a significant share of a city's total amount of some crime type. By treating the stream of crimes as a symptom of one underlying problem in need of repair rather than as a series of unrelated demands for traditional police responses, officers, property owners, and other residents have devised creative, effective solutions, such as special lighting in convenience store parking lots or checkpoints around bars at closing time that interdict both drunk drivers and illegal weapons.

The recommendation's emphasis on involving the community in cleaning up hot spots adds two benefits. First, local residents may have information or insights that create a more effective solution than a police officer or other "outsider" could create alone. Second, the experience of rapid, visible success through collaboration with the police in solving a community problem begins to break down local skepticism about the police and to set the stage for future cooperation.

Two task forces recommended applying the hot-spot approach beyond the crimes for which it has been applied to date—robberies, barroom assaults, and drug market violence. One called for cleaning up hot spots around schools and on heavily traveled routes to and from schools. Asking students where they feel most frightened of violence, then eliminating the threats in those places, might have the side benefit of reducing the fear that drives some children to carry guns to school. Another task force, noting that spouse assaults are among the crimes with the highest rates of recidivism, called for collaboration between family physicians, hospital emergency departments, social service agencies, and police to find and assist families whose homes are potential hot spots for domestic violence.

Reclaiming Public Spaces

Four of the five task forces recommended tactics for reclaiming public spaces in which signs of physical or social disorder discourage public use. Physical disorder is sometimes characterized as "broken windows," but it includes vacant unkempt lots, abandoned buildings, and informal graveyards for junked cars. Social disorder includes not only illegal behavior, such as open-air drug markets, but also nonviolent disorderly behavior, such as groups of young men insulting or threatening passers-by, public drinking, and other behaviors that make people feel uncomfortable or unsafe.

Social disorder occasionally erupts into violence. More commonly, however, social and physical disorder promotes violence through longer term processes. Law-abiding people begin avoiding the "bad" area, wiping out the social networks through which neighbors watch out for one another, keep a watchful but friendly eye on neighborhood children, and generally set a neighborhood tone that discourages crime and violence. Businesses close, removing employment opportunities. Physical deterioration, especially of housing stock, increases the despair and powerlessness felt by residents of these areas, which are also menaced by violence. Conference participants pointed to examples in which these processes had created social and economic vacuums into which violence-prone gangs or illegal markets had spread.

Participants also suggested a wealth of tactics that they or others had used successfully to take back public spaces for public use. These included:

- visible, regularly scheduled neighborhood patrols—in cooperation with police but without visible police escorts;
- neighborhood clean-ups -of alleys, vacant lots, and street corners, especially those that are sites of crime, illegal markets, or social disorder;
- making drug purchasers feel conspicuous as citizen patrols visibly record their license plate numbers, or police stop nonlocal cars for "safety checks" or "warnings" that drivers are entering drug market areas where they may not be safe even though police are watching closely;
- creative "No Turn" and other traffic restrictions during drug market hours to make it harder for nonlocal drug purchasers to cruise past drug markets, much as wealthier residents demand restrictions to keep commuters from taking short cuts through their neighborhoods;
- civic functions operated by churches and other formal and informal neighborhood groups, in places and at times of day or night when drug markets or disorderly groups customarily congregate: examples included lemonade stands, bake sales, ethnic festivals, neighborhood beautification efforts, free rock concerts, sports team autograph signings, and neighborhood block parties;
- city agencies timing disruptive services to coincide with drug market operations wherever and whenever drug markets or other "magnets for violence" are operating: examples included noisy and well-lighted street or sidewalk repairs, installation of speed bumps, repainting street lane markings, tree planting or pruning, checking for gas line leaks, or replacing street lamps (preferably with high-intensity units);
- restructuring the physical environment to make it less conducive to drug markets by enforcing housing codes against crack houses, removing pay telephones from drug market areas (or placing them awkwardly low to the ground), clearing brush and towing abandoned cars from places where they may conceal stashes of drugs or guns, and the like; and
- strategic, vigorous enforcement of laws against underage drinking and public drinking, of alcohol codes against the owners of bars, and of laws governing the disposal of old vehicles.

Participants experienced in the use of these tactics cited the importance of close police-community cooperation. Tactics such as these reportedly present few risks to public safety, and part of their strength lies in being carried out by neighbors rather than by police. Nevertheless, where drug markets are especially well entrenched or violent, police drug raids or street "sweeps" may need to precede efforts by unarmed residents. Even where major operations are unnecessary, the knowledge that police back-up is on call can be important in encouraging community participation in taking back public spaces. In turn, police operations that might be seen as oppressive if initiated by the police become seen as supportive when invited by the community. Finally, adding pressure from the police department to demands from citizens for action by building inspectors, sanitation departments, or other municipal agencies may stimulate a faster response.

Adopting Community Policing

All five task force reports placed high priority on the implementation of community policing. Although there is dispute in policing literature over the resources needed for community policing (or even whether community policing can be defined usefully in terms of resources), community policing initiatives over the past decade appear to have been guided by adherence to four key ideas. First, behind violent incidents reported to police lie problems waiting to be solved, and the best police response is to prevent future violence by understanding and solving these problems.

Second, police should take their cues about what problems are important to solve from the community itself, through face-to-face contacts with residents, through community meetings, and through social observation of the neighborhood, as well as through emergency calls to 911.

Third, arrest should be viewed as only one police response to incidents or problems: offering mediation, using civil litigation and regulatory sanctions, referring people to public or private services, and mobilizing other municipal agencies are other useful responses.

Fourth, the local community is a potentially valuable partner in preventing and responding to violence, but developing that partnership requires constant effort and will experience many setbacks. The historically grounded suspicion of police in minority communities will not be quickly or easily overcome.

Cooperative police-community efforts to clean up hot spots and to reclaim public spaces are in fact exercises in community policing. Although only a beginning, they are building the trust that is essential to implementation of permanent community policing.

Time, resources, technical assistance, and sustained commitment are required. For example, effectively using alternatives to arrest requires both strategic reorientation and specific training for community police officers. Developing partnerships with the community requires not only retraining individual officers, but often reorienting senior and middle management, and above all, allowing time for the community to (re)gain trust in the police as partners.

If police officers on the street are to act on cues from the community regarding priorities, their commanders must give them new delegations of discretionary authority and training in how to use that authority. Developing and implementing those delegations requires senior and middle managers not only to devote significant time for planning, but also to relinquish some of their traditional authority. If community police officers are given nominal authority to mobilize other city agencies to respond to community problems, the entire community policing program will be undercut unless the other agencies are reoriented to act swiftly in response to the officers' requests. Part 4 reports one task force's vision of how such a reorientation might look.

As noted above, the federal government could advance conference participants' apparent unanimous goal of community policing by structuring the delivery of resources for new police officers (e.g., provisions in the pending crime bill to increase police) so as to help and encourage jurisdictions to adopt this model. In doing so, however, it will be important to be vigilant regarding the potential hazards and costs associated with community policing. One hazard is that discretion may open the way to greater police corruption and preferential service. The costs include the need for more officers and the possibility of slower responses to emergency calls because officer mobility is reduced.

Objective 3: Reduce violence hazards in communities.

Many task force recommendations were intended to reduce community hazards for violence. In the public health model of violence prevention, violence hazards are places or situations that regularly bring together elements that increase either the probability that violence will occur or the consequences if it does. Two examples are fixing hot spots and reclaiming public spaces, discussed above. In addition, the participants made recommendations dealing with the three most recognized elements of violence hazards—firearms (especially in the hands of youth), alcohol, and illegal drugs—and with a variety of other elements.

Controlling Firearms

Although research reviewed in *Understanding and Preventing Violence* suggests that firearms add little to the total number of violent crimes, the case fatality rate—the fraction of injuries that lead to death—is much greater when guns are used, and the severity of nonfatal injuries caused by guns far exceeds those by any other weapon. All five task forces made recommendations intended to reduce the substantial contribution of firearms to the number of murders and the enormous costs associated with firearm-related injuries. Several task forces called for public debate on various federal actions that they thought would make that task easier:

- passage of the "Brady Bill" 5-day waiting period for handgun purchases [which subsequently occurred];
- a national ban on sales of assault weapons;
- closer regulation of firearm dealers;
- nationwide confiscation of unlicensed handguns;
- increased federal taxes on guns and ammunition to cover the societal costs they cause;
- tort liability of gun manufacturers for the costs of injuries and deaths caused by use of their products as directed;
- more effective federal law enforcement to stop interstate gun dealing; and
- elimination of export subsidies for firearms.

Recognizing that one mayoral task force was likely to have little influence on national firearms policy, the task forces devoted most of their discussion of firearms to local policy: new laws and sanctions, enforcement priorities, and public education efforts that Cornet City itself could take. Each recommendation was intended to accomplish at least one of the following objectives: to reduce violent gun uses; to reallocate guns away from high-risk users, especially unsupervised juveniles; to reduce the number of guns flowing into Cornet City; or to reduce the lethality of guns flowing into Cornet City.

Three general features of the recommendations seem both politically and ethically important. First, they reflect a belief that unsupervised gun possession by juveniles in a city is rarely beneficial and frequently devastating. Second, with few exceptions, they focus on punishing behaviors that are already illegal; they involve minimum coercion of law-abiding adults, including gun owners and purchasers; and they attempt to stop negligent or criminal acts through which guns reach the hands of unsupervised juveniles. Third, in general, participants said these recommendations should not be announced by mayors or other public officials; rather, they should emerge from informed public debate. As one mayor expressed it:

> [In encouraging neighborhood forums], the mayor should say, "We want to have strategies to make neighborhoods safe come out of neighborhood forums. Think broadly. Consider all types of things . . . You should debate whether we should have a [gun] confiscation program similar to the sobriety check point."

> And if a neighborhood said, "Yes, indeed, this is what we'd like to do," and if we could get it to pass constitutional muster, then the city should be allowed to confiscate weapons in those target areas for a limited period of time.

Reducing Violent Gun Uses   Two approaches to reducing violent gun uses were suggested by some of the task forces, although there was not opportunity to explore their full ramifications: allowing waiver of juveniles over 14 years old to adult court for felonies involving deadly weapons, with provision for incarceration in separate age-appropriate facilities; and selective police use of portable metal detectors to deter illegal carrying of concealed weapons.

The first recommendation, a reduction in waiver eligibility age, was recently enacted by the legislature of Colorado, whose statutes already prescribed enhancements to adult felony sentences for use of a gun. The reduction in waiver age was to expose juvenile offenders to the same sentence enhancements. The task force that made this recommendation did so on the condition that, as in Colorado, juveniles waived to adult court serve their sentences in a special facility devoted exclusively to this population.

The second recommendation grew out of a recognition that concealed guns add to the risk that a violent encounter will end in murder or permanent disability. The task force proposed that the mayor consider two tactical approaches for the random use of metal detectors. The first would involve conventional detectors placed strategically in public access areas (schools, libraries, subway entrances) that would deter individuals from carrying guns. The detectors would be redeployed regularly. The second would involve an elite, highly trained police unit that would randomly employ portable units at key points. If the detector is activated, the police would make a search and confiscate any illegal weapons. The primary purpose of the random searches, however, would not be weapons confiscation, but rather to create a deterrent effect.

Participants' support for such a program seemed nearly unanimous, but there was explicit concern that it emerge from the local community, that it be implemented constitutionally, and that, because its purpose would be to deter illegal carrying rather than to apprehend illegal carriers, it should be implemented only following wide publicity.

The task forces could not carry out a full constitutional analysis of the recommendation, but several points were noted. Probable cause or permission is required if using the metal detectors requires more than "minimal" intrusion. If the suspect must be "stopped" in order to conduct the search, probable cause is required. Several cities have encouraged citizens to call in tips that "'X' is carrying a gun at . . . ," then interpreting the tips as probable cause to stop "X." The success of these programs seems to depend on building trust between community residents and police.

Without probable cause, the constitutionality of searches for guns hinges on whether the scans involve no more intrusion than being approached by a drug-sniffing dog in an airport, which has been found constitutional. A comprehensive constitutional analysis of these and related matters would be useful to jurisdictions considering this approach. The same questions arose in connection with a related tactic: gun confiscation checkpoints in conjunction with sobriety checkpoints, at which police look for guns as they ask a few questions and smell drivers' breath. With current technology, detecting guns inside a vehicle that are not in plain view apparently requires more than the minimal intrusion permitted by the Constitution. Again, however, the task forces did not have the benefit of a comprehensive legal analysis.

Reallocating Guns Away from Juveniles   The task forces noted the concentration of murders of youth by youth, and several decided that any benefits of allowing unsupervised urban youth to carry guns were outweighed by the risk that these guns will be used in murder. They therefore called for consideration of new laws and new law enforcement priorities to reduce this risk:

- a ban on unsupervised juvenile gun possession, including such severe penalties as incarceration in a specialized age-appropriate facility, plus a suspended adult sentence, plus a term of probation;
- a stringent local firearm dealer licensing requirement that includes criminal record checks and requirements to do business from a fixed location built to prevent thefts;
- a ban on gun sales to minors in Cornet City;
- a "safe storage" ordinance requiring owners to store their guns in places inaccessible to children; and
- stiff sentence enhancements for burglary and fencing when the stolen property includes a gun.

Current federal law already prohibits federally licensed gun dealers from selling guns to minors. Available data suggest that violations by licensed dealers with fixed places of business account for very few of the guns used in juvenile violence. In calling for new laws, the task forces intended to shift some of the burden from law-abiding dealers to minors by prohibiting them from unsupervised possession of guns, and to plug some of the other channels through which guns flow to minors. These channels include: purchases without proof of age from persons who obtain federal licenses but sell guns on the street rather than out of fixed business locations; purchases by adults for resale to minors; personal purchases from nondealers, which are unregulated in many locations; theft or unauthorized "borrowing" of parents' guns; and purchases of stolen guns from burglars or fences.

The task forces understood that the proposed laws would not be easy to pass or enforce, since they involve large numbers of "retail" transfers involving one or two guns rather than concentrated "wholesale" transactions by a few kingpins. However, they recognized that the debate over passage would offer a chance to educate Cornet City residents about the risks that the guns they purchase to protect themselves may wind up being accidentally discharged by their children at play, used against a loved one during a heated family argument, used by their child against another child, or stolen and passed into the black market. And, while proactive enforcement of the laws would prove difficult, severe punishment of the suppliers of guns used in violent crimes could be expected to deter at least some future violations.

Two task forces called for two law enforcement initiatives against illegal activities that increase both juveniles' demand for guns and their access to them: crackdowns against violence around schools and other places youth congregate, to reduce the fear that motivates them to carry guns; and law enforcement crackdowns on trafficking in stolen guns, illicit markets for guns, and barter in guns for drugs.

Reducing the Number of Guns   One task force called for both new laws and public education activities to reduce the flow of guns into Cornet City: restrictive licensing of handguns, with no provision for "grandfathering in" handguns already owned; and public education to mobilize the community against selected dealers who sell the guns most frequently used in youth violence and to communicate the dangers of guns in urban settings. Participants believed that the campaign to enact the licensing reqirement and the public education effort would be mutually supportive.

Reducing the Lethality of Guns   One task force called for several measures to lessen the threat to public safety posed by guns that do enter Cornet City: requiring combination trigger locks on guns sold in Cornet City; a local excise tax on ammunition, with rates especially high on the types of ammunition most frequently used in violence; and a law making gun manufacturers liable for the costs of injuries and deaths in Cornet City resulting from use of their products according to directions.

Reducing Alcohol Abuse

The task forces generally accepted two themes of *Understanding and Preventing Violence*: that alcohol is a drug and that violence frequently follows alcohol abuse. This orientation led to a call for long-term development of more effective substance abuse prevention programs and to more emphasis on alcohol in such programs. More immediately, the task forces recommended several steps for reducing alcohol-related violence in Cornet City—especially violence that occurs in homes or involves youth:

- mobilizing joint efforts by the city government, community residents, news and entertainment media, and alcohol sellers for public education campaigns to reduce underage drinking and encourage responsible adult drinking;
- targeting liquor stores, convenience stores, and bars that violate licensing and sale-to-minors laws for policing, regulatory action, and community protest as a threat to health and safety;
- periodic driving-while-intoxicated (DWI) checks at closing time at drinking establishments, publicized in advance so that their primary effect is to discourage alcohol abuse rather than to increase DWI arrests;
- police attention to the frequency of alcohol abuse at scenes of domestic violence and a policy of police referral for alcohol abuse treatment as needed, even when a criminal justice response is unwarranted or impossible; and
- greater use and enforcement of alcohol abuse treatment as a required postrelease sentence condition for persons convicted of violent crimes.

Interrupting Illegal Drug Markets

One of the four task forces explicitly adopted the position stated in *Understanding and Preventing Violence* that while alcohol-related violence is associated with heavy drinking and other forms of alcohol abuse, violence associated with illegal drugs occurs in the marketing. The other task forces seemed implicitly to have adopted that view by including illegal drug markets, along with other hot spots, for which the community and police would need to plan and implement violence prevention strategies.

The task force that explicitly discussed violence related to drug markets expressed its position as follows:

Drug markets are peculiar to location. Problem-solving community policing (rather than sweeps of addicts or general buy-and-bust operations) is to be the primary law enforcement response to these markets [in Cornet City]. Crack house by crack house, block by block, the police are to work with residents and merchants affected, to analyze the conditions that permit the market to flourish, to agree to a plan to eliminate those conditions (including, of course, arrest of sellers and use of law enforcement power to get addicts into treatment), and to prevent the market's return to the location. The assumption is that we will waste our law enforcement resources (and our prosecution, court, and correctional resources) unless they are brought to bear in this location-specific, problem-solving way and unless both the community and the police commit resources to preserving the gains and protecting the location for a considerable time thereafter.

That task force discussed alternative approaches to the entire drug problem: "medicalization," legalization, and decriminalization, but did not develop any agreed-upon suggestions on those broader questions. Recognizing its own inability to reach agreement, and the fact that national drug policy should consider a host of drug-reated problems besides violence, that task force simply encouraged the Cornet City mayor to foster broad debate and discussion of those alternatives at the national level. Like the other task forces, however, this one recognized that those charged with urban violence reduction "will carry a very heavy load" until the demand for drugs decreases and joined several others in calling for expansion of drug treatment capacity and improvement of drug abuse prevention technology as methods of violence prevention.

Reducing Other Violence Hazards

The various task force reports called for a number of specific measures to alleviate violence hazards in Cornet City that were only peripherally associated with firearms, alcohol, and illegal drugs.

Expanding Secure Emergency Shelters for the Homeless   One task force noted that violence occasionally erupts among groups of homeless persons on the streets.

Scattering Public and Assisted Housing   In concentrated areas of public housing, the ratio of youths to adults is too great to permit effective supervision. If public housing is dispersed, it reduces the clustering of unsupervised children and adolescents.

Building Safety and Livability in the Design of Public, Commercial, and Residential Buildings   The violence prevention effectiveness of "defensible space" appears to depend in part on the routine activities and kinds of social interaction of the people who occupy that space. All buildings, including public housing, can be designed and built to encourage social interaction.

Finding and Fixing Open Spaces that Present Hazards for Violence   As noted above, reclaiming public spaces can be an important violence prevention approach. Police can walk through neighborhoods, following typical pedestrian traffic patterns, to locate potential havens for violence—such as parks and recreation centers isolated from heavily traveled areas; abandoned houses and commercial buildings; berms, hills, and small woods that may shelter drug dealers; concrete "canyons" that cannot be seen from nearby windows—and making structural changes, or at least adding patrols, to improve public safety.

Setting Up a Demonstration Alternative Dispute Resolution Center   Such a center, particularly in a high-violence neighborhood, might be a means of interrupting the escalation of disputes into violence.

Creating an Interagency Violent Death Review Board   The task of such a board—including staff of the medical examiner, police, corrections, emergency medical services, social service agencies, schools, an epidemiologist, neighborhood "old heads," and other appropriate community representatives—is to conduct an epidemiological review of all murders, to identify patterns of preventable deaths and to design specific preventive procedures. This approach has successfully reduced fire deaths in Milwaukee and teenage drug overdose deaths in Washington, D.C.

Teaching First Aid to Youths   Youths are particularly good targets for first aid education for two reasons: they are more likely than anyone else to be present when a youth is stabbed or shot and therefore might save lives, and the training may sensitize youth who experience violence primarily through entertainment media to the real-life threats and other consequences of violence.   Fire Department slack time and resources might be used to undertake this activity.

Objective 4: Strengthen supports for children and their families.

As noted in the Introduction, one fundamental theme that emerged from the conference was the recognition that families have a basic responsibility to protect their children from the risk of growing up as violent children and adults, but many families need help to meet that responsibility. Therefore, all the task forces discussed what help government can provide to families and how it can best deliver the needed support.

One mayor explained the problem as follows. When a child or youth is recognized to be at risk of violent behavior, or to have committed an act of violence, "services need to be driven by the family as the unit [receiving services], not by the child or [some other] individual member as the unit." Research cited in all the reports discussed at the conference shows clearly that violent youths are likely to come from families with violent siblings or parents; with members who abuse drugs or alcohol; with parents who lack childrearing skills and access to support services; or with other problems, such as low income, poor housing, or inability to function in a complex urban society. More likely, the troubled family is suffering from several or all of these problems simultaneously and therefore needs a variety of supports.

A basic difficulty in supporting troubled families is that they are discovered by, and the necessary services are typically delivered by, a complex, uncoordinated network of service providers, scattered across a host of uncoordinated local government departments and private organizations. A family seeking a variety of services must discover and apply for each service in a different location, following different rules, often providing redundant documentation, and often involving different family members. In accepting the needed services, the family surrenders control to a variety of different eligibility requirements and standards for accountability, instead of being helped to take more control of family life.

Creating Family Resource Centers

As an organizational means of recognizing families as the appropriate intervention units, integrating service delivery, and strengthening the role of families in identifying their needs and planning tailored solutions, several task forces called for creating Family Resource Centers. As described by some speakers, such Centers might resemble turn-of-the-century settlement houses for new immigrants.

A family resource center must include a family service coordinator, designated to signify the role as coordinating services on behalf of a family rather than managing the family as a case. The service coordinator would work with a family in developing an individualized problem-solving plan and to mobilize providers of all the needed services, whether their organizational location be in a government agency, under an independent school board, or in a charitable organization, church, community development corporation, or elsewhere. Third, the centers would have space-sharing by service providers, to facilitate "one-stop shopping" in settings that are convenient to public transportation, offer child care, and minimize other barriers to service utilization. Fourth, trained staff (e.g., counselors, social workers, and registered nurses) at the center would be available to provide emergency support for abused and neglected children, battered women, witnesses to violence, and others in acute need. Fifth, the centers would provide coordinated outreach to troubled families as they are discovered by schools, community organizations, welfare agencies, community police officers, the juvenile justice system, probation officers, pretrial services agencies, or other neighborhood residents. Sixth, with informed family consent, the service providers would share information. And, finally, the family service coordinator would be authorized to monitor service delivery and require correction of problems.

The task forces recognized that implementing such a plan for family resource centers would require significant changes in the agencies that are most likely to come into contact with troubled children and their families. Specifically, several task forces called for two organizational changes: reorientation of child welfare services from deterrence and separation of families toward prevention of the child abuse and neglect that makes separation necessary; and full-service schools.

Reorienting Child Welfare Services

Conference participants recognized that child abuse and neglect are evils both in themselves and as contributors to future violent behavior by the child victims—a conclusion of *Understanding Child Abuse and Neglect*. Sadly, separation of a victim from the rest of the family is sometimes the only solution. But two of the task forces urged that this drastic step become a last resort, to be undertaken only in cases for which intensive prevention efforts have failed.

Making prevention the first step will require a significant reorientation of child welfare services systems in many localities, including, it was believed, in Cornet City. The goal would be to identify and solve family problems before a child is injured, physically or psychologically, and before parents' inability to manage marital conflict and anger without violence imprints damaging images, and teaches patterns of violence, to the children.

Various task forces called for several steps to make prevention a priority: assisting mothers *and fathers* (including stepparents and unmarried domestic partners) gain the skills needed to raise well-behaved children who respect life and to manage their own frustrations and anger without resorting to violence; identifying sources of conflict and other problems in the home; locating natural helpers (e.g., grandparents, extended family members, godparents) who show an interest in the child and maximizing their involvement in solving the family problems—before taking official action; and preparing an inventory of sources of help in the neighborhood and drawing on those sources—when they meet specific needs, with family permission, and before taking official action.

Concern was raised that the call for programs to offer "parenting training" may be ill-advised, since there is little evidence to show their effectiveness. Low-income families are especially difficult to reach for such training. Also, research suggests that some parents who respond poorly to their own children respond positively and consistently to other children, showing that the problem may not be lack of skills.

Child welfare service agencies were urged to consider the public health model of violence prevention and to establish strong working ties with the local public health agency in order to prevent child abuse and neglect. Two promising models that begin prevention work even before a child is born are discussed in *Understanding Child Abuse and Neglect*. The Prenatal/ Early Infancy Project in Elmira, New York, and its replications in Denver, Colorado, and Greensboro, North Carolina, involve regular home visits by nurses for expectant mothers and their families in the months preceding and following childbirth.

In Hawaii's Healthy Start Program, home visitors sponsored by the state's Department of Health regularly visit families of newborns. Both programs target high-risk families, provide a range of services (maternal education, parental training and counseling, teaching routine health care for infants, ways to discipline without corporal punishment), and provide occasions for the mother to engage in pleasant, supportive social interactions.

At least in the short term, both programs appear to improve family functioning in ways that reduce rates of child abuse and neglect in high-risk families, although only the Prenatal/Early Infancy Program has been subjected to rigorous evaluation. As health programs, these interventions also expand families' access to primary health care, nutrition, and substance abuse prevention for expectant mothers, which improves fetal neurological development; and training in the prevention of head injuries to infants and children. These health services reduce risks of damage to children's neurological functioning—damage that, by reducing their abilities to learn, think, and communicate, set them on life courses that tend to end in violence.

Creating Full-Service Schools

The task forces were keenly aware that in many neighborhoods afflicted by violence and other social problems the schools are among the most viable remaining social institutions. Therefore, they called for enlisting schools in supporting children and families in ways that may reduce violence. In the words of two task forces:

> The schools must see themselves as part of the neighborhood rather than primarily as part of the larger school system. We want them to work in partnership with neighborhoods, the recreation department, the churches, and community agencies to enhance children's experiences and the quality of community life.

Various task forces developed lists of specific programs that full-service schools should consider offering. These included services that parents might want for their children, with the expectation that parents come to school occasionally, too—to learn about offerings that they might choose to help themselves be better parents. The programs included:

•   "Safe Passage" programs, in which school counselors, teachers, parents, and police, cooperate to identify threats to children's safety on the way to and from school and to eliminate those threats;

•   staggered opening and closing hours, so that younger, smaller children travel between school and home while older, stronger children, including school bullies, are expected to be in class;

- "Safe Havens," places in which children, their families, teachers, and supportive residents (such as mentors, service providers, members of the business community) feel safe to give and receive services and support, beyond traditional school hours;
- peer mediation programs for students and training for parents in mediating family disputes;
- a K-12 curriculum to teach children nonviolent conflict resolution skills (New York City's Resolving Confict Creatively Program was suggested as one model, but programs are more likely to succeed if they are tailored to local conditions);
- recreational opportunities such as midnight basketball, to give teenagers alternatives to hanging out on the streets;
- programs for training and supervising interested high school seniors in tutoring younger students, as a constructive activity for the tutors and a means of preventing early-grade school failure; and
- space at which day care could be provided, by trained staff assisted by neighborhood volunteers, to the children of students and other neighborhood children.

There was a belief that this list is only a beginning—that success by full-service schools in delivering a few of these programs would prompt suggestions from neighborhoods for a wealth of additional services that would benefit children, families, and therefore, the whole community.

Developing Other Community Services

Beyond the reach of child protective services and full-service schools, the task forces recommended other programs and services that the mayor of Cornet City should consider for helping children and families prevent violence:

- alternative schools, beginning at the elementary level, staffed by teachers and professional counselors with specialized knowledge of children with behavior problems, using Americans with Disabilities Act funds to support services for children whose problems stem from cognitive or communicative disorders;
- youth aid panels following the Philadelphia model, in which a citizen board is set up to identify youths whose behaviors are problematic for the community but do not warrant criminal justice action, to recommend community service restitution and monitor the youths' performance;

- programs for gang youth and "wannabes," to deal with fear, loneliness, boredom, and other problems that encourage youths to join gangs;
- linking children who witness violence on the street and in the home to emergency and rehabilitative mental health services; and
- fostering the development of day care partnerships, involving willing neighbors as much as possible, as a means of supervising children while single parents are at work.

One more category of recommended supports for children, intended to help them make the transition from school to work, is discussed under Objective 6, along with other investments in human capital.

Objective 5: Reduce violence in the home, which is both a problem in itself and contributes to violence on the streets.

The support systems discussed above for children and their families should help to prevent violence in the home by reducing well-known risk factors, including family members' anger and depression, stresses that weigh especially heavily on single-parent families; alcohol and illegal drug abuse; social isolation; and family disorganization that tends to accompany poverty. However, recognizing the importance of violence in the home as both a problem in itself and a contributing factor to future violent behavior by children, several task forces called for programs intended specifically either to prevent family violence or to detect it and respond when it does occur.

Nurses' home visits, already recommended, were cited as a promising approach to preventing violence in homes, at least in the short term. Other recommended strategies rest on the repetitive nature of violent attacks on family members. Because family violence is among the most recidivistic of all violence, detecting one incident usually offers an opportunity to prevent future incidents involving the same individuals. Therefore, the task forces called for two immediate steps to detect and interrupt chronic family violence.

First, analyze all domestic violence police calls received in the past 6 months, identify high-risk homes where the pattern suggests continuing and escalating violence presents an imminent risk, develop a plan tailored to specific conditions in each high-risk home, and carry out the plan—an extension of the hot spot concept to family violence. Second, secure from the Housing Department as much temporary shelter as is needed to provide safe havens for women and children at imminent risk of battering.

Although these were seen as useful immediate steps, the task forces put a high priority on creating a permanent referral system, which, it was believed, could be put in place within a few months as part of a three-part short-term agenda. First, set up a centralized Family Violence Referral

Network—a referral network through which police officers, health care providers, teachers, social workers, pastors, advocates, neighbors, and others who find women and children in danger of battering can refer them to a system of safe shelters in convenient but concealed locations, designed and planned to make them as inviting and simple to use as possible. Second, analyze available data on compliance with protection orders and, if necessary, develop or revise operating procedures for monitoring compliance. Third, train medical and social services and hospital emergency departments to recognize, treat, and report suspected violence against adult and child family members.

Participants recognized that these measures will not succeed in preventing all family violence. Therefore, one task force called for criminal justice sanctions to punish batterers with sanctions that were firm yet tailored to solve specific family problems. The first recommendation was to create a "domestic violence protocol" that contemplates any of the following sanctions when they seem useful and appropriate: issuance and enforcement of restraining orders, obtaining safe havens and psychological services for victims, providing to perpetrators anger management training and substance abuse treatment when those appear useful, and sentencing perpetrators to prison when that appears useful. The second recommendation was to create a Domestic Violence Court dedicated to cases of violence in homes and authorized to implement the domestic violence protocol and monitor and enforce compliance.

Objective 6: Rebuild human and financial capital in communities weakened by violence.

Despite widespread agreement on the importance of violence prevention, conference participants repeatedly expressed concern that preventive resources in high-risk urban neighborhoods would eventually be overwhelmed unless the young men living there became better connected to the mainstream economy. As one mayor put it:

> [Current conditions] feed just the opposite of the principle that the benefits of working have to exceed the benefits of crime . . . There is no functioning economic market place in the conventional sense in most of our tougher neighborhoods. It doesn't work if we think that somehow we can change people's behavior [without one]. They are rational folks, and they understand this mix.

Another mayor emphasized the circular connections between economic opportunities, the criminal justice system, preventive interventions, and violence:

> We are spending a lot of money—not as much as we should but a lot of

money—to invest in community development: housing and economic commercial development. And yet we buttress the money that goes into development with virtually nothing in terms of law enforcement...[not just adding] police, but things like Town Watch, intervention groups, and other things that do have an impact...

But . . . it all comes down to one thing. I think we are kidding ourselves if we talk about all of the things that we've just talked about, including stronger law enforcement, if we don't talk about job opportunities. We could have the best schools, . . . the best training, . . . [but] unless you can redirect job opportunities to where the people at risk live in this country, we're out of luck. We're going to change nothing. We can have the best health system, . . . we can have peer mediation, . . . but unless you give us the ability to have job opportunities for people as they come through the school system [and] get into the job market, it is not going to matter.

The task force recommendations for connecting young community residents to job markets fell into three categories: increasing human capital, the personal skills needed in the legitimate economy; linking individuals to appropriate existing opportunities; and increasing the financial capital needed to expand employment opportunities in minority neighborhoods.

Participants believed that it is essential to begin work simultaneously on all three categories. Young people lack incentive to increase their skills if they expect those skills to go unrewarded. And the skills will go unrewarded if fear of violence discourages entrepreneurs from expanding opportunities in the neighborhoods where low-income minorities live.

Increasing Human Capital

The full-service schools and alternative schools described above contained a number of features that would increase children's capacities to participate in the legitimate economy. In addition, the task forces called for four less global initiatives:

• expand programs modeled after "I Have a Dream," but broadened to offer financial incentives for high-school students to pursue *either* specialized vocational training or college-level academic work after graduating from high school;
• enrich school programs for high-risk youth, especially by updating vocational education course offerings, to develop skills needed to enter the modern work force;
• develop programs modeled after Boston's City Year and Harlem's Youth Build, local service program models that give youth needed skills and engage them in a year of community service; and
• develop systems for identifying and serving youth and young adults

under juvenile or criminal justice system supervision who need help with reading deficiencies, alcohol or drug dependence, poor life-management skills, or other obstacles to employment.

Linking Individuals to Opportunities

Several task forces recognized that some young minority men are unemployed not because of inadequate skills or lack of opportunities, but because of barriers, including discrimination and lack of information, that keep them from being linked to those opportunities. Their recommendations for removing these barriers included:

- use the mayor's "bully pulpit," the urgency of the violence crisis, community action, and financial incentives to promote nondiscriminatory hiring practices and to encourage the hiring of minority youth;
- subsidize corporations for training new employees from high-violence neighborhoods in job- or employer-specific skills—perhaps working through the local Private Industry Council and tapping Job Training Partnership Act funds; and
- promote business/school partnerships.

Programs such as the "Pathways to Success" have shown considerable success in motivating children to remain in school and facilitating their transition from school to work—while indirectly combating the problems of idleness and hopelessness. This type of program is an American variant of the successful German apprenticeship programs described in *Losing Generations*. In such programs, the business community offers summer jobs and one-on-one mentoring apprenticeships to teach useful skills (both job-specific and pertaining to the general world of work) to expose children to productive role models, and, it is hoped, to counteract negative stereotypes that employers may have of minority youth. Schools participate by teaching necessary skills and facilitating access to the internships or apprenticeships. To motivate participation, the youths are guaranteed part-time and summer employment so long as they remain in school and meet academic performance requirements.

The juvenile justice system could also participate by channeling selected delinquents into the program. "Pathways to Success" would also incorporate some features of "Adopt-A-School" programs, such as employee leave time for in-school mentoring, youth training in entrepreneurial skills, donations of used computers, and other aids to improve the employment prospects of minority youth.

Increasing Financial Capital in Minority Neighborhoods

Conference participants recognized the importance of creating jobs in cities. As one mayor put it:

> In the cities, [we don't need] the employment playing field to be leveled. We need the employment field, which is now tilted radically against us, to be tilted radically for us.

Several participants seemed skeptical, however, about traditional methods of accomplishing the tilt. They recognized that the increasing concentration of voters in suburbs had dimmed the prospects of major infusions of federal money into cities. For two reasons, they doubted that tax subsidies for locating enterprises in targeted high-risk neighborhoods would create jobs there: fear of violence was thought likely to neutralize the effect of any tax incentive, and recent research findings suggest that even when firms are drawn to minority communities by tax incentives, they hire local residents only when required to do so.

Several task force members lamented the lack of business community representation at the conference, thinking that members of that community might have produced creative ideas for attracting financial capital to Cornet City and its high-violence Southwood neighborhood. Nevertheless, those present suggested several tactics:

• monitor compliance by banks and other lenders with Community Reinvestment Act requirements for investing in inner cities;
• create a Community Development Corporation (CDC) to consolidate available investment funds and invest them in promising new ventures that would employ local residents;
• promote economic activity that connects youth to the labor market—for example, a local housing rehabilitation program that employs local youth— perhaps as a public-private venture, a CDC venture, a Youth Corps project, or an initiative supported by the Commission on National and Community Service;
• form an Industry Council to produce and carry out a long-term economic development plan, as a way to increase the local tax base and revenues available for antiviolence programs and to produce decent jobs that will strengthen families and neighborhoods while providing good role models for youth; and
• broaden contracting opportunities for minorities.

One scenario was suggested for the third tactic, promoting economic activity in Cornet City. The first step was to seek federal funds, free from overly inhibiting regulations, with which to create businesses that would employ large numbers of teenagers at public works projects. Later, the city could lobby for legislation requiring state agencies to buy maintenance, painting, and other services from these special enterprises—knowing that city subsidies will be needed to close the productivity gap between them and their experienced competitors, but recognizing that the city may reduce its future violence costs by providing labor market experience to its youth. One participant wondered whether a federally seeded State Revolving Loan Fund, or special incentives to pension funds, might encourage the initial investments needed to launch special enterprises.

Two mayors pointed out "zero-cost" ways that the federal government could create jobs for residents of minority communities. One way is to locate new federal facilities in urban areas, which would provide job opportunities; the mayor noted that compliance with an executive order of the Carter administration would accomplish this at no cost because the funds were to be spent anyway.

The second mayor noted that Clinton administration plans call for tax subsidies to firms that locate new facilities in enterprise communities and empowerment zones, provided that 50 percent of new employees live in the zone and that one-third of them have been previously unemployed. He recommended an additional step for increasing the impact of the zones:

> [Require that] 10 percent of all federal procurement must come from firms within enterprise zones . . . Businesses would be stampeding to get into those zones because there is nothing like federal procurement. We can tag in city procurement . . . and maybe state procurement.

Another participant reminded the group that while the procurement suggestion had merit, it would probably not be totally free because subsidies might be required to cover the productivity gap between zone enterprises and firms that produce the same goods now.

Another mayor talked more broadly about federal policies that affect urban economic development. In his words:

> You should stop forcing capital into the high end of the housing industry. The federal tax law does that. We're the only country in the world with "master bathrooms." Because of the [mortgage interest write-off with no cap], you have these huge houses being built, and increasing percentages of the investment in housing are going into fewer and fewer houses at the high end of the market. You might want to talk to Canada about that. They have a tax system that is neutral across [all levels] of housing.
>
> The other thing I wanted to mention is . . . the tremendous damage that was done by the federal government over the last four decades in encouraging the ripping out of transit systems and building these huge Autobahns—even Hitler didn't put Autobahns in the middle of cities! That only happened here. I think that . . . this administration understands this enough to do . . . what is right for cities. A transit system as extensive and wonderful as Philadelphia's . . . would really do a lot to centralize the

economy and provide jobs in the middle, where people who need them the most can get at them.

Noting that these are only two examples of federal programs that have had unintended adverse consequences on urban communities, one conference participant suggested that a requirement for "community impact statements" analagous to environmental impact statements might help prevent future damage.

Objective 7: Promote a prosocial, less violent culture.

There was a pervasive sentiment among conference participants that a "violent culture" promotes violent behavior, especially among young people. A principal goal voiced by all conference participants is changing community norms that accept or promote violence. Unfortunately, two institutions with a powerful influence on culture—religion and the entertainment media—were unrepresented at the conference. Therefore, discussions about how to accomplish the goal were abbreviated. Conference participants including researchers were uncertain about both the mechanisms through which cultural influences promote violence and how to change the nature of these influences. Furthermore, they recognized the fundamental importance of constitutional limits on state power to promote religion or regulate media content.

Nevertheless, one task force recommended long-term steps the federal government might take to reduce violence-promoting effects of the entertainment media and to use the media in campaigns to discourage violence: consider the level of violence-promoting material, and citizen complaints about such material, in processing applications for broadcast license renewal; develop voluntary partnerships with the media to engage in more vigorous and proactive antiviolence public service campaigns, and sponsor randomized trials to evaluate the effectiveness of such campaigns in different communities and geographic regions; and sponsor the development of media literacy programs that teach children to question violent entertainment material.

In addition, several task forces called for immediate steps by the mayor of Cornet City and other local officials to encourage religious organizations, entertainment media, and other cultural institutions to assume voluntarily their shares of responsibility for preventing violence: use the "bully pulpit" of public office to charge all elements of the community with the mission of violence prevention; discourage public and private actions that aggravate ethnic tensions or promote negative, violent stereotypes; enlist celebrities in voluntary antiviolence campaigns; and encourage the media to publicize early successes in responding to violence.

Using the "Bully Pulpit"

As a follow-up to declaring Cornet City's violence out of control, one task force urged its mayor immediately and publicly to charge the entire community with moral responsibility for preventing violence, using whatever resources they possess. That task force challenge used the following words:

> Official agencies will have a lot to do in implementing the Antiviolence and Violence Prevention Program, but it is critical that Cornet City be reminded powerfully of the central roles that will never be performed by [government]: the actual rearing and protecting of children, the instilling of values that support health and personal safety, and the passing on of a commitment to (and knowledge about) nonviolent ways of handling anger and conflict.

> These [roles] are to be attended to by families, however defined; by churches; by neighborhoods; and by the [institutions] whose support, guidance, and discipline sustain them. Mr. Mayor, we encourage you to charge them as well.

> Press pastors to open their churches to new uses that permit formation of new supports for struggling single parents: respite centers for beleaguered single parents, hot meals to draw families together [to hear offers of support services of various kinds, such as] training in management of households, conflict resolution, discipline, and child development.

> Press for churches, schools, and any other plausible facility to establish voluntary respite centers, to which parents can go for a spell when they fear losing control of their children (or their temper), and where they can expect to find other parents or volunteer "godmothers" and "godfathers" from whom to seek advice, with whom to share the burdens, or with whom to leave their children for an hour.

> Call for families to have weekly meetings to work through the risks of violence (or becoming violent) that they face in the family, in the neighborhood, at school. You probably won't get laughed at, you'll go some distance in reminding people of their own roles and responsibilities, and maybe there will be less carnage on Family Meeting nights.

> Call for businesses and city agencies to provide as an employee benefit training in parenting and household management for employees from the time of pregnancy.

> Call for businesses to offer employees two hours a week to volunteer to work with youth, and prepare the Department of Parks and Recreation to organize volunteer opportunities. Other city agencies, too.

> Press adults to look out for their neighbors' children, and to take some responsibility to help and—yes, interfere, if that's the word—when an unsupervised child (yes, a teenager, too) is putting himself or herself at risk.

Variants of this message can be delivered by elected officials at all levels of government and of all political stripes. Like all political messages, the credibility and effectiveness of this one depends on strategic selection of audiences, places, and methods of delivery.

Increasing Sensitivity to Negative Stereotypes

One task force recommended that Cornet City's mayor take two actions to reduce the violence-promoting effects of negative stereotypes of young minority males: sensitize government press officers and other staff to actions—speech mannerisms, treatment of city agency clients, for example—that may aggravate ethnic tensions or promote stereotypes of young minority men as people to be feared, and call on the community to take actions against billboards, movies, concerts, and other vehicles that portray violence, underage drinking, and related negative behaviors by young minority men as "cool," "macho," or justified by oppression.

These recommendations reflected two concerns: first, that violence, and its uneven distribution across society, feeds a stereotype of young minority men as people to be feared rather than led into adult society and charged with adult responsibilities; and, second, that the stereotype itself promotes violence in two ways. Some young African-American and Latino men may limit their own legitimate economic opportunities after learning that a menacing demeanor and willingness to use violence offer "power" while academic, vocational, and social skills are "white" and useless for minorities trying to get ahead. At the same time, whites for whom the menacing stereotypes justify discrimination in hiring make the media portrayals a reality by driving young minority men, regardless of skill level, out of the mainstream economy into illegal markets that reward their abilities to threaten and use violence.

Enlisting Celebrities in Antiviolence Campaigns

Beyond reducing antisocial messages and negative stereotypes, interest was expressed in ways to enlist celebrities and advertisers, voluntarily yet quickly, in emergency responses to "out-of-control" violence. Advertisers of popular brands of tennis shoes and other items that occasionally become objects of violence can be encouraged to sponsor high-profile, prime-time public service ads against violence, starring their celebrity endorsers. The "We Are the World" approach, involving extraordinary collaboration and a spiritual context, was mentioned as potentially useful. Locally, athletes and other community heroes can make personal appearances and pleas to abandon violence.

Some participants cautioned that such campaigns could backfire without careful matching of celebrities, messages, and audiences. As one person put it: "If the plan is for Pat to make speeches against urban violence, you better make sure that Ewing, Moynihan, and Robertson get to the right auditoriums."

Publicizing Successes

Concern was expressed that two kinds of successes may be underreported in news media. First, some community-based efforts are succeeding in reducing violence in their communities: publicity about such successes rewards the efforts of those responsible; it may also encourage other readers to become involved. Publicity about activities and successes will be especially important in the first days and weeks after official recognition of a violence "crisis."

Second, some participants expressed a sense that "bad" statistical news about violence receives more media attention than "good" news, thereby increasing harmful fear and despair over violence. For example, it is unlikely that many people realize that the national murder rate dropped by about 5 percent between 1991 and 1992 or that the murder arrest rate for black males aged 25 and older had been nearly halved since the early 1980s.

Although public officials have no direct control over media content, one task force recommended that Cornet City's mayor use personal appearances at scenes of successes, background briefings, and press conferences to publicize local success stories, to publicly recognize the leaders responsible, and to highlight encouraging statistical trends in violence.

4

Organizational Issues

As task force and plenary discussions produced the portfolio of violence prevention interventions summarized in Part 3, four concerns surfaced repeatedly: costs, the need for local organizational changes, changes in the relationships between different levels of government, and the need to evaluate programs and keep an open mind concerning what works. This final point deserves special emphasis because knowledge about what interventions work—and under what circumstances—is very limited.

Discussions of these four topics were less definitive than discussions of interventions. Nevertheless, participants suggested that reducing violence will require initiating some innovations without full knowledge of their probable consequences, then refining them as consequences become clear. Both scarce resources and organizational incentives must be directed to support this innovation strategy, sometimes called "Ready, fire, aim!"

Elements of this strategy include intervening on a small enough scale to limit risks to acceptable levels, so that fear of failure doesn't paralyze action; doing enough advance planning to develop a threshold level of consensus and to innovate with awareness of operational realities, but not enough to lose the sense of urgency about reducing violence; and incorporating an evaluation mechanism just secure enough to maintain a degree of accountability and sensitive enough to signal needs to modify the intervention, but not so elaborate that it stifles or diverts the innovation. As one speaker put it:

Just as we protect society from [ineffective] and harmful [medications] by first testing them and measuring their effects, we ought to be assessing our social programs for safety and efficacy before accepting them as [universally] effective. We can learn about the causes of violence by learning how to reduce it.

The remainder of this part discusses ideas that emerged from the conference about resources, innovations in local government organization, and new intergovernmental links needed to support action against violence.

The Cost of Controlling Violence

The task forces received no guidance in how to treat budget constraints. As a result, they recommended interventions with a wide range of costs. However, all task forces implicitly accepted the constraints now facing all levels of government and focused more attention on ways to better use current resources rather than on suggesting major new spending initiatives. A consistent refrain was for federal and state governments to loosen the reins and give local officials more discretion to mobilize resources to fit the needs and priorities of their cities. Many ideas called simply for new ways of approaching problems and, it seemed clear, would cost little, if anything. Other recommendations seemed likely to require substantial investments, while the costs of others would depend on program participation levels that are difficult to predict. Still others would actually save money by reducing incarceration costs, which are among the fastest growing items in state budgets.

Acknowledged uncertainty about costs and savings raised the needs for two approaches: develop preliminary estimates or estimation methods for the costs and savings of the selected interventions recommended in Part 3, and develop a voluntary system and repository for exchanging information about actual experience with costs and savings and update the preliminary estimates and methods accordingly.

Local Government Reorganization

Several Part 3 recommendations involve major organizational innovations, such as community policing, family resource centers, and industry councils. Successful implementation of such far-reaching organizational changes will require resolving difficult management questions and rebuilding—or simply building—community trust. Several task forces noted that such basic reorientations rarely happen quickly. They seemed unlikely to happen at all, in fact, unless the Cornet City mayor's response to the violence crisis included an urgent push to begin them and sustaining that push even after public opinion moved on to other concerns. Otherwise, it was feared, agencies would gradually drift back into protecting the traditional bureaucratic interests of mandates, budgets, and standard procedures.

One task force recommended that the mayor use the current crisis of violence in Cornet City to engage the attention and commitment of all city agencies to reorganize local government services around the needs of the city. To manage the reorganization, it urged the mayor to establish and fully authorize an Interagency Working Group chaired by the deputy mayor.

Although no standard approach will fit all cities in need of reorganization, it is useful to recount the task force's description of the Interagency Working Group in some detail as an outline of the kinds of issues to be addressed in reorienting local government so as to counteract forces that promote violence. In the words of the task force:

> The guiding mission statement of the Interagency Working Group is that the city government and the community of Cornet City will re-enforce and re-establish peace, stability, community values, and the sense of opportunity in the community. But it will pursue this mission by focusing primarily on what it can influence—police, schools, housing, recreational facilities, health services, and economic development—rather than on what it cannot.
>
> The Working Group will focus on neighborhoods as the unit of delivery and analysis, it will utilize community organizing and organizations, and it will see partnerships—with the private sector, with nonprofit agencies, with other levels of government, and with community grassroots efforts— as critical to its success. The religious community will be an essential partner. Churches and synagogues bring to an important part of the community the message of individuals' obligations to the community. They also offer volunteers, "neutral territory," and facilities for meeting and working together and access to other organizations.

To ensure that all agencies remain committed (and that their operational concerns surface early during the reorganization), the task force recommended that the Interagency Working Group members include the deputy heads of all city operating agencies, along with local planning and budget offices. Deputy heads of all relevant community organizations would also be invited to join.

To conserve resources, manage risk, and provide a learning opportunity, it seemed best for the Interagency Working Group to implement government reorganization in pilot neighborhoods first, before introducing the most successful and generalizable innovations citywide. This particular task force proposed choosing three pilot neighborhoods—one in crisis and two in need of preventive efforts—believing that this approach would produce more generalizable approaches and a stronger constituency for change than would pilot testing only in neighborhoods in crisis.

The Interagency Working Group would design government reorganization by responding to needs as they are identified by the three pilot neighborhoods. In addition to representing his or her city agency, each Working

Group member would serve on the "neighborhood desk" for one of the pilot neighborhoods. The desks would be responsible for planning responses to needs identified by residents of its neighborhood, mobilizing all city services as needed.

Each pilot reorganization would begin with information gathering through a survey and other methods. It would follow community organizing principles and outreach to include as many residents as possible in meetings with the relevant city officials. These meetings would be a primary vehicle in each pilot neighborhood for creating the alliances needed to promote effective citizen-government interaction. Each agency would be expected to organize such meetings, perhaps on its own but preferably in concert with other agencies. Agencies should be prepared to respond with at least modest resources to some of the problems identified by the community. Agency heads should be warned that negotiating solutions will not always be a quick or smooth process, especially in neighborhoods in which residents have no previous experience with a government that they believe is interested in them, and so patience will be needed. The meetings should be organized to allow necessary venting of citizens' frustrations, followed by setting priorities and developing solutions to specific issues on a business-like basis, so that both the community and government officials gain a sense of progress.

While the Interagency Working Group and its board works toward long-term restoration of trust in Cornet City's government, it should also focus on providing tangible signs to all parts of the community that prompt, effective action is being taken against violence. The Working Group should be empowered to take quick actions on such matters as lighting, fencing, police visibility, and protection of children on their way to and from school. Quick responses on such matters are signs that the city is beginning to take action. They are facilitators of, but not substitutes for, the more important long-term response.

As reorganization proceeds in the pilot neighborhoods, it will solve some problems with available resources. However, it is also likely to discover underlying problems that demand new resources, and to spawn community organizations that could, with modest financial support, contribute substantially to community solutions. To fund needed interventions and to assist promising community organizations, the mayor's office should designate a grants officer to draw on federal grant programs, foundations, and other private sources of funds.

New Intergovernmental Relationships

The conference produced no calls for massive new federal financial assistance to reduce urban violence. Instead, most of the discussion of assistance focused either on nonfinancial forms of federal and state assistance or on delivering current levels of financial assistance more flexibly.

Providing Nonfinancial Assistance to Local Governments

Some forms of federal assistance other than financial grants that participants recommended have already been discussed, especially in connection with firearms and with urban economic development. Other forms of assistance and approaches were called for by the mayors and others during the closing plenary session.

The importance of the expanded earned income tax credit (EITC), progress toward universal health care, and other actions to reduce welfare dependence were cited by mayors as among the most important actions the federal and state governments can take in reducing urban violence. By increasing worker mobility, making urban residents feel more secure, and increasing personal prosperity in cities, these measures have an enormous impact in mitigating the social pathologies that foster violence.

One mayor called for federal law enforcement to concentrate on reducing interstate crime (especially drug and firearm trafficking), rather than expanding the domain of federal law enforcement into local violent crime. The federal government should also produce and disseminate a catalogue of federal assistance programs that can be used to support antiviolence initiatives and community-based organizations. Similarly, it should produce and disseminate a catalogue of available technical assistance and information about operational experience with antiviolence initiatives.

Providing Flexible Financial Assistance to Local Governments

In various ways, all of the mayors and many task force participants lamented obstacles to flexible local use of categorical federal funds to meet a broad range of family and neighborhood needs and to deliver services through the smallest possible geographical unit. As one mayor put it:

> [First], as we go up the channel [from local government to] state government to federal government, often the regulations and the details and the categories become more [specific], when as you go up in level of geography they should become more general.
>
> Second, . . . we ought to explicitly say that these programs need to encourage risk[-taking]. Right now they encourage control, accountability, auditing, programmatic requirements. They ought to be built in ways to encourage [taking] . . . well-intended . . . risk.
>
> [Finally], HUD is the only federal agency, I think, that recognizes a city exists . . . Justice no longer recognizes cities, they only recognize states. HHS no longer recognizes cities, it only recognizes states . . . So as we try

to chase HHS dollars up, we're . . . trying to figure out revenue streams and then fight with the state bureaucracy. It's impossible to configure services in a comprehensive way. And Justice then has block grants and discretionary grants.

Another mayor summarized the problem as follows: "We need [federal assistance] in a way that is tailored to local needs, and federal response should be based on a local strategy."

No task force, mayor, or federal official present was prepared to specify in detail a mechanism for delivering federal financial assistance in a way that allows local officials sufficient flexibility in selecting from a comprehensive array of services to produce assistance "packages" tailored to the specific needs of individual families. However, several speakers sketched pieces of a delivery system intended to accomplish this purpose. The pieces described included: encouraging regional offices of federal agencies to waive categorical requirements whenever necessary to facilitate flexible local use of assistance; establishing "city desks" to help localities acquire funds from programs across the federal government and marshal them to meet locally identified objectives; transplanting the service integration model from public housing projects to entire neighborhoods; and borrowing from delivery systems for other forms of assistance.

Waiving Categorical Requirements Several speakers in the closing plenary concurred in the need to authorize regional officials to waive categorical requirements of federal aid programs when needed to allow local officials to meet shared goals. The discussion suggested that while senior HUD officials, at least, were committed to such flexibility, additional work was needed to get the regional offices "on board" with a waiver program.

Establishing City Desks One mayor praised the idea of creating federal agency "desks" for particular cities:

The person that ran that desk . . . would obviously have an enormous amount of interaction, not just with government officials but with the neighborhood leaders and community leaders, and get a feel for the specific problems and specific needs of an area . . . A good portion of the federal funds that come into your city are available to go into streams that are most [urgently] needed . . . That flexibility would be wonderful. I don't know if it can be achieved.

However, one federal official reminded the group that organizational approaches resembling city desks were tried in the Model Cities Program during the Johnson administration. He doubted that allocation of aid from multiple departments and agencies through a city desk for every city needing help was administratively workable, and suggested: "We've got to figure out how to take that idea and sophisticate it so that we get something that is responsive and that works."

Integrating Services One mayor suggested that the service integration model of public housing assistance offered an example of how to configure assistance with the necessary flexibility:

> There is this service integration around the family unit in public housing, where we have connected community policing with public housing. You have grants for public safety. You have grants for economic development. You have grants that require resident participation in configuring services . . . So we have an example. Now the problem . . . is it only works within the four walls of public housing. It makes sense in terms of how you think inside HUD, but [to] those of us who are trying to deal with neighborhoods, . . . it's a relatively hard official geographic designation.
>
> So I think the answer is really quite simple. If we combine welfare reform with family-oriented, family preservation service delivery models, and we . . . have the funding streams be more comprehensive, becoming . . . more specific as they go down, and match these up in something like the public housing model but on a geographically more sensible scale, I think we can do it.

Borrowing from Other Delivery Systems One participant raised the need for alternatives to the "social R & D" model, in which program ideas are raised, embraced as promising, evaluated in pilot tests, then mandated for adoption everywhere. Concern was expressed that that model takes too long to be workable. Alternative promising approaches may be suggested by several examples of federal-state cooperation:

• Federal Emergency Management Administration: Federal funds are sent to localities for rapid distribution by local authorities, a response that is quick but provides virtually no accountability in terms of fairness or effectiveness.

• Justice Department support of the civil rights movement: During the 1950s, the department sought information throughout the South about local groups that were undertaking local initiatives, provided support to those that showed promise, facilitated information sharing, and allowed public opinion about effectiveness to emerge without formal evaluation.

• Agricultural Extension Service: The Agriculture Department supports a network of locally stationed technical experts, who make validated information freely available to those who request it.

• disease treatment and prevention: The National Institutes of Health and the Centers for Disease Control and Prevention disseminate recommended protocols for treating and preventing disease, along with a request that doctors voluntarily report on results obtained using the recommended protocol and other approaches, thereby generating an information base for analysis and evaluation.

All participants understood that developing a flexible system for federal assistance to support local innovations for violence prevention would not be easy or obvious. The need for flexibility must be balanced with the need for accountability, through program monitoring and evaluation. But the participants stressed that unless new models are developed, an unacceptably high share of scarce federal aid would be wasted.

Bringing About Solutions As one mayor put it, calls to increase the flexibility of federal aid to localities seemed to be "preaching to the choir" at the administration level, in view of steps that were already being undertaken, but: "At the congressional level, though, we've got a mountain to move because . . . [consolidating programs] means the elimination of the subcommittee . . . that monitors a particular program."

It was believed that gaining statutory changes to increase flexibility would require a much broader discussion, including members of Congress—not as committee and subcommittee chairs but as representatives of their states and congressional districts. Analogously, engaging state legislatures and governors in aligning state statutes and programs to meet urban needs would be important. Distinguishing restrictions that are wedded to deeply held policy convictions from those that are not will require serious and statesmanlike engagement by governors, state legislatures, and the Congress.

Conclusion

The consensus of the conference participants was that violence must be recognized as threatening the core values of national life—tearing away the confidence and sense of community that are essential to an open society. They warned that violence is a complex phenomenon, fed by diverse sources. Creating the conditions for a more civil society will require sustained and significant efforts of both the public and private sectors.

Violence in Cornet:
A Case Study

U.S. Department of Justice
Office of Justice Programs
National Institute of Justice

National Institute of Justice

Violence in Cornet:
A Case Study

by
Patricia Kelly

**With contributions from
Jeffrey Roth, Ph.D.**

Prepared for the National Institute of Justice, U.S. Department of Justice, by Abt Associates Inc., under contract #OJP-89-C-009. Points of view or opinions stated in this document are those of the authors and do not necessarily represent the official position or policies of the U.S. Department of Justice.

The National Institute of Justice is a component of the Office of Justice Programs, which also includes the Bureau of Justice Assistance, the Bureau of Justice Statistics, the Office of Juvenile Justice and Delinquency Prevention, and the Office for Victims of Crime.

LIST OF EXHIBITS: PART A

1: Homicide, 1980 - 1990.

2: Percent Arrestees Testing Positive for Drug Use, 1986 - 1990.

3: Drug Use Among Victims, 1985 - 1988.

4: Robbery, Burglary and Drug Violations, 1980 - 1990.

5: Weapons Used in Homicides, 1980, 1985, 1989.

6: Map of the City of Cornet

7: Clearance Rates for Part I Offenses and Drug Violations, 1983 - 1990.

8: Homicide Circumstances, 1980, 1989.

9: Homicide Rates for Black and White Males, 1980, 1985, 1989.

10: Major Causes of Death in Cornet, 1980, 1985, 1990.

11: Murder Assailants Under the Age of 18, 1986 - 1990.

12: Relationship of Victim to Offender

13: Cases Dismissed Due to Evidence Problems, 1974, 1990.

14: Cases Dismissed Due to Witness Problems, 1974, 1990.

PART A: THE PROBLEM

A. THE MURDER OF ANITA WOODS

There were 12 shots: six in rapid succession; a pause; and then six more. Lydia Davis reached for the phone and dialed 911. There was a recording.

> *"You have reached the Cornet City Police Department. All of our operators are currently handling emergency calls. Please stay on the line and your call will be answered. Thank you."*

Davis was not surprised that the line was busy. She had called the police on a number of occasions and this was not the first time she had gotten a recording. She was mad, however. How on earth could the emergency number *ever* be busy? The message was repeated 5 times before an operator answered. "Hello, how may I help you?"

"Gunshots in the 700 block of Forten Street, NW." Davis said wearily.

"How many gunshots, ma'am."

"Twelve, I think."

"We'll send someone right away."

She hung up. Davis called her neighbor, Martha. "Did you hear those gunshots?" she asked.

"Yeah. I can see whoever it is lying in a pool of blood right across the street from my house. I'm tellin' you, Lyd, I don't know how much more of this I can take." Martha Heywood lived on Forten Street, the main hangout of the neighborhood's drug dealers. There were times when Heywood was kept awake all night by the constant traffic: cars driving up with their stereos blaring, dealers shouting to one another, the sound of bottles breaking. She was glad that at least she was retired and didn't have to get up for work the next day. She would get her sleep before noon, when the next shift of drug dealers began appearing.

"I'm coming around in a minute," Davis replied. She pulled on a jogging suit over her pajamas and grabbed her coat. As she was locking her door she saw other neighbors walking toward Forten Street, one block north of them. Davis was a 46-year-old office administrator who was relatively new to the neighborhood, having moved there 10 years ago.

This section of Southwood, called Poplar Hills, was populated by middle-income African-American families who had initiated the area's racial "turnover" in the 1940s. Poplar Hills was a mixture of semi-detached and row homes with small lawns and porches. The turn-of-the century residences had recently attracted a handful of young whites to the area, including college students looking for cheap housing away from the State University's main campus. However, the white population was still too small—and too 'poor,' in relative terms—to cause any real gentrification of the neighborhood. There was still a "small town" air in Poplar Hills, a sense of everyone knowing everyone else—which, indeed, they did. It was one of the things that attracted Lydia Davis to the place. She had never imagined that there was a drug problem in a neighborhood where small vegetable gardens could be found in many backyards, and a tricycle forgotten on the front lawn overnight went undisturbed.

"Here we go again," she said to herself, "we all come out here after there's been a shooting. We shouldn't be living this way. We know who these boys are. We know what they're doing. We shouldn't put up with this. We shouldn't." Davis joined a crowd of people standing a few yards away from the body.

"Who is it?" she asked her friend Martha.

"That Woods boy's sister." Mark Woods was 19 years old, and the youngest of four children. He and his sister Anita lived with their grandmother several blocks north of Forten Street. Mark was one of about a dozen neighborhood youths who hung out in front of a string of abandoned businesses on Forten Street, stepping up to cars to make unhurried drug sales. He was a 'lieutenant' in the street hierarchy: an intermediary between the local supplier and the boys and young men—and a few females—who made the actual drug transactions. It was clear from the way he carried himself, and the way others treated him, that he was powerful.

"Why on earth would they kill Anita? She wasn't dealin' those drugs, was she? I thought she was just usin' drugs. Are they starting to kill their customers now?"

"Maybe the ones who don't pay up," someone in the crowd commented drily.

"Or maybe they tryin' to get back at the brother," said Mr. Leonard Francis, who lived on 6th Street, a few houses down from Davis. "Gettin' back at him for something he did, through her." Francis was a retired government employee who was active in local politics. He had recently been elected the representative for Section 4C10 in the Southwood Civic Association.

"I don't care what the reason is, it don't make no sense."

Lydia turned to Mr. Francis. "Maybe we should form one of those neighborhood patrol groups like they have out in Northwood. We have enough people, don't you think?"

Francis shifted uneasily. "Yeah, sure, that would probably be all right."

Davis was dismayed by his tepid reaction. He was one of the most outspoken people at all the community meetings, talking about how we shouldn't wait for the police to do things, we should take the matter into our own hands. But he had never tried to form a citizens' group.

"We too old to be out here standin' on the corner against these boys. You see how ruthless they are. What makes you think they're gonna pay attention to us?" This comment was from Hattie Mason, a retired school teacher who also lived on Forten Street, two doors down from Martha Heywood.

As Davis stood there, listening to her neighbors, she began to feel increasingly frustrated. Why couldn't they all band together and try to do something? Of course, some of these people were the parents or grandparents of the children who were tearing the neighborhood apart; it wouldn't be surprising if they were against a patrol group. But what about the others?

The young woman who had been shot was loaded into the ambulance. Her brother Mark, the drug dealer, was pacing angrily, his eyes glassy with tears. "I'm gonna get 'em," he kept saying, his teeth clenched. "I swear I'm gonna get 'em." His friends stood nearby, hands deep in their pockets.

B. A WEEKEND OF VIOLENCE AND THE GOVERNMENT'S RESPONSE

The next morning, the death of Anita Woods made the front page of the *Cornet Courier:*

Six Slain in Weekend Murders
Victims Include 3-Year-Old

In the city's bloodiest weekend this year, six people died under circumstances ranging from child abuse to robbery.

On Friday evening there was an emergency call to an apartment in the Southwood section of the city, where police found a 3-year-old girl on the livingroom floor. The child had broken bones and multiple skull fractures, and was pronounced dead at the scene. Frank Cartwell, the common-law husband of the child's mother, was taken into custody. The mother has not yet been located.

In a second domestic matter a woman was shot by her estranged husband as she left her apartment. The previous week Teresa Cordoba had tried to get her husband arrested for threatening to kill her. A restraining order had been issued, according to Superior Court officials.

On Saturday night a convenience store clerk was shot twice in the head after being robbed by two men. Sung K. Suk, father of the slain man and the store's owner, witnessed the murder. He said that his son had offered no resistance. "He had given them [the] money and he was on his knees with his hands on [his] head. But the guy stood there. . . shot him point-blank. It was really brutal."

Early Sunday morning an argument in the parking lot of a local bar left one man dead of multiple knife wounds. His assailant, Lawrence J. Peterson, also was wounded during the altercation and is listed in stable condition at the County Hospital. Patrons of the Hitching Post said the fight started when Peterson and the deceased, Michael Harrington, tried to leave the parking lot at the same time and had a minor collision. This was the third violent altercation at the bar so far this month.

A 17-year-old restaurant employee who was fired last week returned to his former place of work and opened fire on employees in the kitchen. The restaurant's owner was killed and several employees were wounded, one seriously. The youth, whose name is being withheld because of his age, fled the scene but was later arrested at his home.

Finally, 22-year-old Anita Woods was gunned down in the 700 block of Forten Street, in an ageing section of Southwood known as Poplar Hills. CCPD detectives report that they have no motive at this time. . .

The article provoked a political firestorm; city officials were deluged with calls from citizens demanding action. Commissioner Willie Farnsworth, chairman of the Public Safety Sub-Committee, said that his office alone received 300 calls within hours after the story was published. "The people who have been calling my office are just fed up. This violence is getting totally out of control, and they want something done about it," he said, "we have got to get these criminals off our streets.

"I have been calling for a tougher approach to law enforcement for years, and maybe now the mayor will listen. This latest bloodbath makes it clear that the criminals control our city, and we need to take back our streets from them. I am calling once again for reinstatement of the death penalty. We also need to lower the age when you can try as adults these young thugs out here who are literally getting away with murder. We are living in extreme times, and we need extreme measures to bring this situation under control.

"We've also got to have longer sentences to keep these violent criminals in prison, where they belong. Let's give the streets back to the law-abiding people. We've got it backwards right now—it's the good people who are locked up in their homes, and the criminals who are roaming the streets freely. This has got to be rectified. The people of Cornet deserve better, and I hope that the City Commission is ready to do what's necessary to stop the insanity in the streets."

In his oblique criticism of the City Commission, Farnsworth was targeting Martin McCafferty, chairman of the Commission's Human Services Sub-Committee. McCafferty was often pegged as the Commission "liberal" because of his voting record on the "law-and-order" issues—particularly his efforts for stringent gun control. He, too, made a statement to the press.

"It is easy to get emotional when these kinds of tragedies occur, but we need to look at the facts. In four of the six murders we had this weekend, guns were used. One of them, I believe, was a young man who, in a fit of rage, went home and got his father's gun to kill his boss. The only reason that that man is dead, and the only reason the other people in the restaurant are in the hospital today, is because the young man had access to a gun. That's the only reason. The way to stop the carnage is not just to say we're gonna lock people up after they've already killed someone. The answer is to take away the means to kill. We are not going to eliminate homicides in this city, but at least we'll prevent a lot of them."

The mayor's office also was swamped with telephone calls and even a few telegrams from angry citizens. By the end of the day, mayor Chris Warren had called a press conference. Flanked by the Deputy Mayor and the Chief of Police, Warren read from a prepared statement.

"This weekend's spate of murders in our city has been a wake-up call for all of us. I have heard from every group in the city: the old and the young; working and retired; male and female; black and white. I have heard from the citizens of Northwood, and those of Southwood, from the business community and from government workers. The citizens of Cornet agree, and I am in full accord, that *something must be done*. This city— indeed, this nation—is awash in blood. It must stop.

"Today, I am charging 12 people to come up with a plan in 100 days to deal with the problem of violence in Cornet. The members of the Anti-Violence Task Force will be: Police Chief Tony Burnett; two of my colleagues from the Commission, Willie Farnsworth, who chairs the Public Safety Sub-Committee, and Susan Wolfe, chair of the Tourism and Economic Development Sub-Committee; the Honorable Connor Bradley, senior judge in the Juvenile Court Division; David Silver, chief prosecutor; Thomas Eckert, Commissioner of Prisons; Stephen Balliet, President of the Chamber of Commerce; Samuel Lee of the Small Business Association; Sheila Robinson, Commissioner of Public Housing; the Reverend Aaron Weems; and Dr. Gail Hodges, professor of urban studies at the State University. Chairing the Task Force will be Deputy Mayor John Canady."

The duties of the Task Force were threefold: first, to attend community meetings throughout the city to get firsthand knowledge of the nature of the problems faced by different constituencies, and to gather information on effective grassroots initiatives. Second, the Task Force would hold citywide public hearings to obtain testimony from "experts" as well as local citizens. Finally, the Task Force had to review the history of anti-violence and anti-crime initiatives before developing a strategy. They could also evaluate efforts in other states, as well as any national programs and policies.

"This Task Force will look at the causes for the skyrocketing homicide rate, and it will develop concrete solutions. I am authorizing and requiring that they mobilize every member of this city, from the grassroots level to the government bureaucracy. Every one of us has got to be a part of this effort, because crime and violence are the number one problems facing this city and this nation. Violence affects everyone, and stopping the violence has got to be everyone's priority."

C. THE VIEW FROM THE POLICE DEPARTMENT

After the press conference Chief Anthony Burnett got into his car and returned to the office. He felt a little subdued. More than anyone else, he knew that violence was now a commonplace in Cornet. Although he wanted to see an end to the problem as much as anyone else, it worried him that such an important public policy issue was taking place in a highly-charged, politicized context. There also would be intense pressure to solve the six weekend murders. Burnett used his car phone to call Deputy Chief Jerry Rauss.

"Hello, Jerry, this is the Chief. I'm calling about this Task Force thing. Yeah, it's going to be hell. Listen, I want you to call each of the precincts where those six weekend murders took place, and tell them that we're sending our best homicide detectives to their areas and I want full cooperation from everybody. Next, I want you to call down to ODA [the Office of Data Analysis] and tell them to bring me everything they've got from 1980 to now on homicides: number of people, motives, weapons used. Everything. I want to meet first thing tomorrow morning."

1. The Office of Data Analysis

ODA was located in a large room shared by Jack Newman, the Director; Sylvia Patton, a Research Analyst; a data entry clerk; and a secretary. There were printouts everywhere, and boxes of papers were stacked in every corner. Newman and Patton had stayed late to get the Chief's data. They walked into his office the next morning with a sheaf of documents.

"Well," Newman began, "including the death of Anita Woods this past weekend, a total of 452 have died in Cornet this year." "If this keeps up, we'll have another record-breaking number of deaths. We've only got a population of 600,000 so if this continues, our homicide rate will rival that in urban areas like the District of Columbia, Chicago and New York City."

"That's a distinction we definitely don't want," the Chief replied. ODA data showed that, after several years of decreasing homicide rates, in 1985 the number of murders in Cornet began to climb precipitously, from 148 in 1985 to more than three times that number by the end of 1990. (See Exhibit 1.) More than half the victims were black, mirroring national trends.

Exhibit 1:

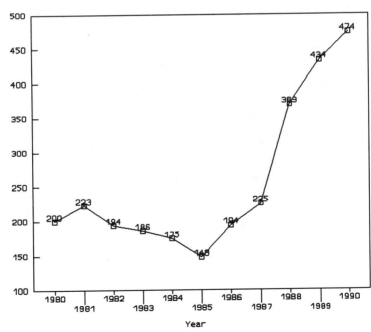

HOMICIDES IN THE CITY OF CORNET

1980 - 1990

Exhibit 2:

PERCENT ARRESTEES TESTING POSITIVE FOR DRUG USE
1986 - 1990

	1986	1987	1988	1989	1990
	%	%	%	%	%
Homicide Arrestees Testing Positive for:					
Any Drug Use	44	49	64	35	26
Cocaine Use	25	31	49	32	23
PCP Use	24	25	25	5	3
All Arrestees Testing Positive for:					
Any Drug Use	68	72	73	67	56
Cocaine Use	40	50	64	63	53
PCP Use	39	43	33	17	7

Newman continued. "When you look at the information we're getting—from lock-up, the coroner, the Supplementary Homicide Reports—you see that drugs seem to be the main problem." First, the number of homicide arrestees testing positive for any drug use rose from 44% in 1986 to 64% in 1988 and declined after that. (See Exhibit 2.) In the general population of arrestees—for violent and property crimes—drug use was even more prevalent: a record 73% tested positive for any drug use in 1988, with small decreases observed since then.

A significant number of murder *victims* also had some type of drug or alcohol in their systems at the time of death. Toxicological data for the period 1985-1988 showed that PCP, cocaine or alcohol was found in the bodies of almost two-thirds of all murder victims. (See Exhibit 3.) While the overall fraction of victims using any drug had remained roughly constant over the period, a review of victims' drug use trends showed substantial differences by type of drug:

- victims' use of alcohol, while still among the highest of all psychoactive

Exhibit 3:

DRUG USE AMONG VICTIMS, 1985 - 1988

Substance	1985 No.	1985 %	1986 No.	1986 %	1987 No.	1987 %	1988 No.	1988 %
PCP	23	15	55	27	73	30	26	22
Cocaine	26	17	54	26	70	29	54	45
Heroin	21	14	25	12	8	3	8	7
Marijuana	19	12	60	29	57	24	27	23
Alcohol	59	38	60	29	57	24	27	23
Other	17	11	2	1	12	5	4	3
None	56	35	78	37	93	38	39	32
No. Cases Tested	156		207		242		119	

Source: *Homicide in Cornet City*, December 1988, p. 10.

drugs, had been declining, from a high of 38% in 1985 to 23% in 1988;

- heroin use had fallen by half, from 14% in 1985 to 7% in 1988;
- marijuana use had almost doubled, from 12% in 1985 to 23% in 1988;
- use of PCP fluctuated during that period but was very high, ranging from 15% in 1985, peaking at 30% in 1987 and dropping to 22% in 1988;
- cocaine had become the most commonly used drug, its use increasing dramatically from 17% in 1985 to 45% in 1988.

Next, there were more drug arrests than commissions of either robbery or burglary. (See Exhibit 4.) Starting in 1985 there had been a dramatic increase in the number of drug violations and the following year drug arrests exceeded the number of actual robberies or burglaries. These data did not necessarily indicate that the number of drug-related crimes was overtaking the numbers for other Part I Offenses—only the fact that apprehension rates for robberies and burglaries remained low. Nevertheless, homicides continued to rise even as arrests for drug violations began to fall.

Finally, Newman presented data on murder weapons. "As you can see, firearms continued to be the weapon of choice. Over the last decade, the percentage of homicides involving gun use rose from 62% to 76%." (See

Exhibit 4:

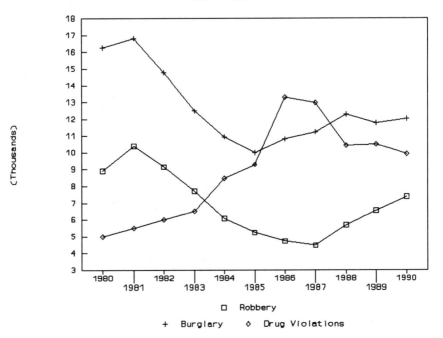

ROBBERY   BURGLARY AND DRUG VIOLATIONS
1980 - 1990

□   Robbery

+   Burglary   ◊   Drug Violations

Exhibit 5.) The Chief recalled hearing one of the Commission members talk about gun control on the previous day, and wondered how the ODA information would be put to use.

Now that he had the big picture, Burnett began to consider the individual cases. Two domestic situations; one robbery with a possible racial component; a disgruntled employee; a barroom brawl. Then there was that young woman gunned down in Southwood.

"I want to be informed on a daily basis about the progress of these cases," he told the Deputy Chief. "The whole city is watching. Use whatever resources are necessary to get the cases solved. Especially that 22-year-old woman, Woods. She's the only one with an unknown motive at this time, is that right?"

"Yes, sir. Detective Soames has been assigned to it."

Exhibit 5:

WEAPONS USED IN HOMICIDES
1980, 1985, 1989

Weapons Used	1980	1985	1989
Firearms	124	95	331
All Other	76	53	103
Total Homicides	200	148	434

2. Investigating the Murder of Anita Woods

Detective Franklin Soames had arrived at the murder scene not long after Anita Woods' body was taken away. In his inspection of the site he found one bullet lodged in the side of the building where the woman had been standing just before she was killed. Several bullet shells were found in the street.

The only other clues Soames could hope to obtain would be from members of the dead woman's family, or people who lived in the neighborhood. He was not at all hopeful that he would in fact get information from any of them. An officer on the scene had told Soames that the girl's brother had been walking around crying, and talking about avenging her death. But the young man had been unwilling to talk to the police and had even dismissed them angrily, spitting out that they were never around when you really needed them. There seemed to be more to his unwillingness to cooperate than just grief, though. Soames discovered that the brother had a record: possession with intent to distribute cocaine. It seemed likely that Mark Woods was a drug dealer and that this was a factor in his sister's murder.

"Very few of the cases I see now are, you know, the typical murders that we were dealing with ten or even five years ago." Soames was speaking to a reporter from the *Courier* who was doing a follow-up story.

"Now there's almost always a drug connection. It's drug dealers beefing with each other over territory. Or it's a dealer killing off a customer who won't pay up—the dealer feels he's got to kill the person otherwise he's gonna be considered a punk [weakling] on the street. And it's really hard to solve these cases because nobody wants to come forward—they can't, really, because then they'd be admitting that they're involved in something illegal. The people on both sides are 'bad' individuals, and there's no incentive for anybody to cooperate."

Soames drove back to his office and stuck a pin in the map in back of his desk. (See Exhibit 6.) Anita Woods' death had occurred in Southwood,

Exhibit 6:

CITY OF CORNET
POPULATION 590,000

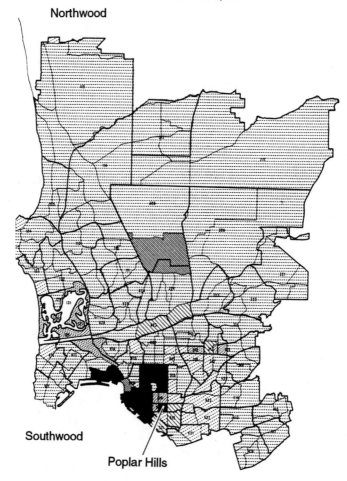

Northwood

Southwood

Poplar Hills

Crimes/1000 Population

- ⊡ 1-15
- ▨ 16-30
- ▨ 31-45
- ▨ 46-60
- ▨ 61-75
- ■ 76-90
- ■ 91 and Above

one of the prime drug-dealing sectors of the city. "Look at this," he said. We've had, what, 450 murders so far? Over half have been here in Southwood." Both geography and demography made the Southwood area a magnet for drug activities, for it was not only the poorest section of the city, it was on the state border, attracting carloads of out-of-state buyers and sellers.

Soames turned his attention back to the Woods murder, and the unlikelihood of getting any evidence to solve it. The families of the victim had no incentive to cooperate with the police, and members of the community faced real *disincentives*. "I know that somebody in that neighborhood—lots of people—know something, or heard something. But I can't get them to tell me. And you know what? I don't blame them. Not really. Because if word got out that they said anything then these people could get killed." Intimidation and murder of witnesses had become so common that when Soames wanted to get information he would never approach the person in public. He knew from personal experience that drug dealers would not hesitate to kill a 'snitch.'

"We're just not dealing with the same kinds of criminals," he lamented. "They will kill people on mere *suspicion* of talking to the cops. I used to tell informants that they didn't have to worry about anything happening to them, but I don't anymore. Because some people I swore to protect got popped. You can't imagine what that does to a police officer, someone who is out there to protect people. When you give people your word, lay down your honor like that and then you're not able to come through. . ." he trailed off, shaking his head. He understood why law-abiding citizens refused to "get involved." He understood their fear because he, too, was afraid.

"I've been on the force for 19 years, and doing homicide for 6 years. When I started out in this job I wasn't afraid, not at all. I mean, sometimes I would be outnumbered by the crooks, you know, but I wasn't afraid because number one, they didn't used to have guns; and
number two, I had this. . . you know, *authority*. I don't mean that I was abusive or anything. Just that people had some kind of respect for police officers. Both the 'good' people and the 'bad' people. Now, though. . . these guys out here are better-armed than I am. Not only that, they're not afraid to kill. Even if you're a police officer." The data did indicate that police work was dangerous, with 138 assaults on police officers in 1990, 13% of them involving a gun.

Without witnesses or other information, it was going to be very hard to solve the Woods case. As shown in Exhibit 7, the police department's closure rate for homicide cases peaked in 1986 at 81%, but by 1990 the rate was only 57%. Clearance rates for other Part I offenses, while lower, had remained virtually constant since 1983, ruling out a general "police overload" explanation. It seemed clear that it was the nature of the murders that

Exhibit 7:

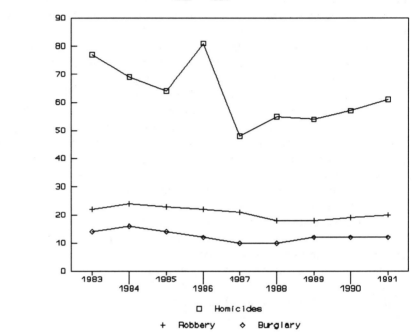

CLEARANCE RATES–PART I / DRUG VIOLATIONS
1983 – 1991

☐ Homicides

+ Robbery   ◇ Burglary

was making it difficult to solve them. "In the old days you had lovers' quarrels, or maybe an argument between friends," Soames explained. "You would usually get the murderer to confess right there on the spot. But now you've got nothing to go on. No witnesses, no anguished parents demanding justice, nothing."

An examination of known circumstances for murders over the last decade supported him. (See Exhibit 8.) In 1980, police were able to determine the circumstances under which death occurred in 75% of their cases, including: arguments/altercations (23%); robbery (19%); domestic disputes (14%); drugs (5%); burglary (3%); and police shootings (3%). By 1989, police were recording the reasons for less than half their cases: only 39% had a known motive or assailant. Even more intriguing, in cases where police could determine neither the reason nor the offender, the majority of victims (76%) were black males between the ages of 16 and 39.

Indeed, homicide among black males was noted with alarm by many groups; these rates were many times higher than that for white males, at

Exhibit 8:

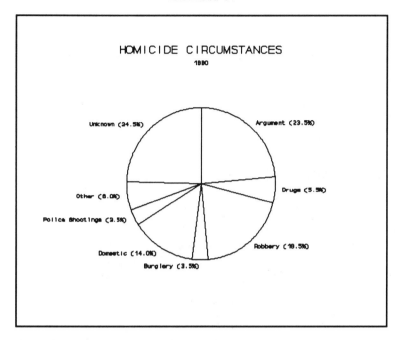

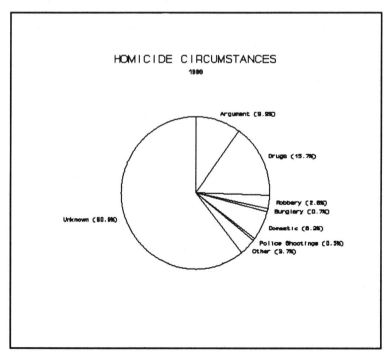

Exhibit 9:

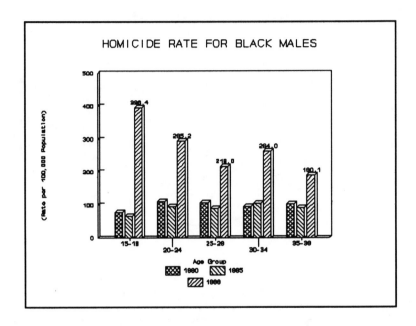

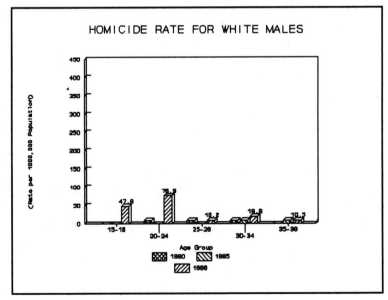

every age. (See Exhibit 9.) In the last decade, homicide had become the major cause of death among black males, particularly young men between 15 and 19 years of age. (See Exhibit 10.) High rates of homicide for other age groups were lower but still significant.

Not only were the victims young, so were the assailants: the fraction of murderers under age 18 had tripled in the last five years, from 6% in 1986 to 20% in 1990. (See Exhibit 11.)

With killers and victims both being so young, journalists often tried to portray the killings as a gang problem. Soames remembered trying to explain the situation to a tabloid reporter a month earlier. "Look, kids do everything else dressed alike and traveling in groups, so they commit crimes and do drugs dressed alike and traveling in groups. But that's got nothing to do with big, formal gangs with initiation rituals, turf staked out, protection rackets, and all the stuff you read about in places like Chicago and Los Angeles. Here in Cornet City, you might have 6 or 8 guys hanging out together for a few months, maybe dealing some drugs or knocking over a liquor store or two. It's serious stuff, but they don't hang together for long, and there's no organized leadership. Maybe we'd have less violence if the

Exhibit 10:

MAJOR CAUSES OF DEATH IN CORNET BY YEAR
Age 15-19 at Death

	Black Males	White Males	Black Females	White Females
1980				
Total Deaths	26	2	10	1
Homicide	18	0	3	0
All Other	8	2	7	1
1985				
Total Deaths	19	2	6	0
Homicide	12	0	2	0
All Other	7	2	4	0
1990				
Total Deaths	84	6	7	1
Homicide	70	5	5	1
All Other	14	1	2	0

Exhibit 11:

MURDER ASSAILANTS UNDER THE AGE OF 18

1986		1987		1988		1989		1990	
No.	*%*	*No.*	*%*	*No.*	*%*	*No.*	*%*	*No.*	*%*
8	6	9	7	26	14	63	19	67	20

kids were better organized. . . they'd work out their own rules so there would be fewer 'beefs' to turn violent. When there *was* a gang hassle that turned violent, you could expect the leaders to work it out like they did after the riots in LA. Here in Cornet City, no one's in charge, so there's no telling what's going to set off a chain of killings, and it's awfully hard to turn things around." Despite this detailed explanation, the day after the interview the headline read: GANG VIOLENCE PLAGUES CORNET CITY, POLICE SAY. "No offense to you, but reporters are really a pain."

Soames worried about all the publicity, and the pressure to solve this murder. Even as he had watched yesterday's press conference, he knew that Chief Burnett would be expecting results. He jotted down a few notes and put them in a file marked "WOODS, A. - 12/11/90." He then began to review his other cases, most of them unsolved. "No, we're just not dealing with the same kinds of cases anymore."

D. THE VIEW FROM THE PUBLIC HEALTH DEPARTMENT

Another person who had watched the mayor's press conference was Dr. William Freis, Commissioner of Public Health. Freis noted with dismay that the mayor had named representatives of all the usual law enforcement perspectives to the Task Force: police, courts, prisons. Only two or three people from the 'human services' view were represented. Freis decided to ask the Mayor and ask to be included on the Task Force.

"Mayor Warren," he began, "there are compelling reasons why I should be part of this initiative. Let me put it to you this way: last year there were roughly 200 deaths from pneumonia or the flu, and almost 200 deaths from diabetes. But so far this year, more people have been victims of homicides than from these other two sources combined. If you consider the flu and diabetes to be serious health problems, why aren't we looking at homicide as a serious health problem? If the public health community is concerned that 458 people died from tuberculosis, which is preventable, we should be just as concerned that an equal number of our citizens are dying from guns, knives, and beatings. These deaths are also preventable. We need to start looking at the problem of violence differently, as a public health issue and not just a law enforcement issue."

Freis was part of a growing movement among health professionals to broaden the definition of public health to "get the topic of violence into the 'mainstream' of public health policy." They argued for a mandate "from the highest levels of government to the individual members of society" to address violence as a health problem that had ramifications for the entire nation. For example, the economic costs of violence include not only expenditures to arrest, try and imprison offenders. They also include medical and psychiatric care for victims; their lost earnings; and, most important, years of potential life lost. It was estimated that homicides and non-fatal violent injuries cost the nation $180 billion dollars in 1990.

In his discussion with the mayor, Freis pointed out that he would like to apply the same epidemiologic procedures to address violence as a cause of death as he would to investigate any other disease or condition. "The issues we need to be concerned with are: who is this 'disease' of violence affecting? What are the risk factors? Where is the violence taking place? Are certain groups more affected than others? What are the circumstances surrounding these deaths? What would be the appropriate interventions for each of these circumstances? These are the things we need to be looking at."

A cursory epidemiological analysis of homicide and violence produced two important observations. First, much of the victimization occurred among black and low-income populations. Freis was concerned that these simple *descriptive statistics* would be interpreted *causally*—as confirming the stereotype that African Americans were more violent than whites. He showed, however, that once one controlled for socioeconomic differences between blacks and whites, the racial differences disappeared. This led him to the view that the real explanation for the high rates of violence lay with poverty and inequality rather than race. It was important to know that the worst consequences of violence were accumulating within the African-American community. But that should not be taken as evidence that African Americans were inherently more violent than whites: they were neither more nor less violent than whites of a similar socioeconomic status.

Second, although a lot of attention was focused on drug-related murders, and in particular the extremely high murder rate among young black males, outside of these special circumstances, most victims were killed by people they knew—very often family members.

"Most family homicides involve spouses and occur in the home," Freis explained. "Citywide hospital data show that when women are killed by the men in their lives, it's usually after many, many assaults. Doctors' offices, clinics and hospitals are a real flash point. They should be considered 'sentinel' points because they offer an opportunity for prevention. When

Exhibit 12:

RELATIONSHIP OF VICTIM TO OFFENDER

Percent of Victims Killed by:	MALE VICTIMS	FEMALE VICTIMS
Spouse/Lover	6%	30%
Other Family Member	8%	12%
Friend/Acquaintance	45%	25%
Stranger	16%	9%
Unknown	30%	27%

Source: *Understanding and Preventing Violence,* NRC, Table 2.6, p. 80 (1993).

we fail to break these cycles of spouse assault, the burden falls back on women."

An analysis of the relationship of the victim to the offender showed that women were more likely to be killed by a spouse, lover or other family member; while men were more likely to be killed by friends or acquaintances. (Exhibit 12.) "You see, the circumstances of murder are very different, so the strategies would be different. A violence prevention strategy for women, for example, might focus on therapy for their partners on anger management, or couples therapy."

And familial abuse wasn't just limited to husbands and wives. The number of Cornet children dying of abuse or neglect had doubled in the last two years: from half a dozen in 1989 to 13 in 1990. The mother was as likely to be the perpetrator as the father. Cornet saw almost 1800 reported cases of child abuse in that same year. At the same time, social service workers could only respond to the most extreme cases: budget cuts in the Department of Human and Rehabilitative Services had reduced the number of child abuse case workers by half. Without the money to hire appropriate staff, the agency had little time for prevention.

Freis concluded his pitch, hoping that his frustration wasn't too apparent. "The fact is, the law enforcement system is not adequately addressing the violence issue. It isn't even a question of giving them more resources, or whatever, because most violent incidents don't pass through the law enforcement agencies. We have battered women in our hospitals who don't press charges against the men who abuse them, so the police aren't intervening there. We see a lot of children with Shaken Baby Syndrome in our clinics. We've got doctors and teachers and social service people who, for whatever reason, aren't reporting suspected cases of child abuse. So the police aren't able to protect that population. Mayor Warren, we can't ignore the fact that the health care system sees more preventable violence, there isn't any reason to wait until there's a homicide for the criminal justice system to step in. Then it's too late. You've got to do more than just get additional cops and longer prison terms. That approach isn't going to reach everybody who needs help."

From a practical standpoint it was impossible to ignore violence as a public health issue because medical professionals were already dealing with the problem. Public medical facilities like the County Hospital in Cornet were overwhelmed, for example, with multiple gunshot wound cases. These patients, many of whom had no health care, were an additional burden in financial as well as medical terms; hospitals were reeling from the large increase in AIDS patients and a poor population that was often forced to use emergency rooms as a source of primary health care.

Freis had one last request. "I *must* tell you Mayor Warren that I'm surprised that someone representing the schools isn't on the Task Force. We need to include the schools in this dialogue for two basic reasons. First, we have an awful lot of violence taking place in the schools. Second, the schools can be part of the solution: they can teach young people about conflict resolution. I think someone from the School Board needs to be represented."

With some misgivings, Mayor Warren appointed Freis to the Task Force. He was worried that the Health Commissioner's prescription would require expensive programs that were no longer feasible in the current fiscal climate. Large funding requests by both law enforcement and social service agencies might force a trade-off between the two approaches, or a compromise where neither of them would get enough money to do anything effectual.

Warren also agreed to appoint School Board President Monica Reeves to the Task Force. He hoped this would end the lobbying for "a place at the table." Warren could not spend too much time worrying about it, in any case. He had to make some immediate decisions about which of many community meetings held throughout the city should be attended by Task Force members, and who should testify at the public hearings scheduled for the next 3-1/2 months. One certainty was that Southwood would be a major focus.

E. A COMMUNITY MEETING IN POPLAR HILLS

Lydia Davis had also been making decisions. After being questioned by Detective Soames, she asked for the name of the local district police commander and, after consulting with several neighbors, arranged to meet him at the local church. Because of the publicity surrounding the death of Anita Woods, this was one of the community meetings that Task Force members had been asked to attend. The prosecutor and Chief Burnett sat quietly in the last pew.

Representing the local precinct was Captain Michael McDougal, a 22-year veteran of CCPD who had found himself attending a lot of community meetings in the last few years. His approach was never to make excuses for the police but to present residents with all of the facts. He began his meeting with Lydia Davis and her neighbors by talking about the lack of resources in the police department.

"I know you probably don't want to hear this, but resources are the number one reason why we can't do as much as we want, and what really needs to be done, in your neighborhood—or any other for that matter. Last month we only had 7 cruisers out of 19 available, because the others were either in the shop or they had been totaled in accidents.

"And then there's the problem with not enough police officers. Every neighborhood is asking for more officers on the beat, more foot patrols. But my number one priority is to make sure we have the ability to respond quickly to a crime in any part of this district. Sometimes I only have half the force available to me at any one time—officers are either out injured, or they're on maternity leave, whatever. If I only have a handful at roll-call I can't put two officers on foot in this area, because if we get a call all the way over on Wyckoff [several miles away] there's no way they can get over there as fast as a squad car."

But it wasn't just cars that were outdated or insufficient in number. The bulk of the paperwork was still being done by hand. There were very few computers and no money available in the police budget to buy more. Indeed, there was no attempt by the top brass at CCPD to develop a strategy to show how and why this new technology would bring efficiency and more time for actual law enforcement. Officers complained that even though they might want to clear a particular street corner of drug dealers, they were reluctant to do so when the arrestee had often paid the fine for "incommoding" and was back on the street before the paperwork had been completed.

Teams of foot patrolmen were sometimes sent out with one walkie-talkie between them. This could be extremely dangerous if they had to pursue a suspect on foot and became separated. Officers complained that Cornet was "in the Stone Age" compared to other cities as far as crime-fighting technology was concerned. In cities on the West Coast for example, they had portable machines which could take fingerprints on the scene and immediately identify suspects with prior criminal records. Cornet officers said there were times when they could not serve a warrant because they could not prove the person standing before them was the one they sought; the suspect, of course, denied being that person.

Resources were especially lacking for the kind of long-term investigation needed to do serious damage to a drug operation. First, there was only a handful of undercover officers available. With so many citizens complaining about street-corner drug trafficking, the police department decided that the high-visibility buy-bust was necessary politically even if it was futile from a law enforcement perspective. At least the police could say that they had made "x" number of raids in a given locality. They could not be accused of "doing nothing." Because CCPD lacked the surveillance equipment necessary for a long-term investigation, officers even used their own video cameras to do police work.

Police officers were frustrated and cynical and so was the public, which felt besieged and frightened not only by the violent criminals but also by corrupt police officers. In 1990 there was an unprecedented number of indictments of police officers, for crimes which included drug distribution, robbery and murder. The increase in criminal cops was attributed to a confluence of factors. First, hundreds of officers were hired in the 1980s without any background check; not surprisingly, many had criminal records. Moreover, a policy change during that time meant that a prior criminal record was no longer reason for disqualification for police work. In addition, both the length of training and its content had been reduced significantly. The combination of youth and poor training was at the root of many of the department's problems. And at the same time that there was an influx of young, inexperienced officers, many of the department's most experienced people were retiring. There weren't enough senior officers around who could be partnered with new recruits. The net result was low morale on the force and a public that distrusted the police and believed it to be thoroughly corrupt. The subject of 'bad cops' was one of the first raised in the meeting with McDougal.

"We got a cop patrols right in this neighborhood, and I swear there's something 'funny' about him," said Leonard Francis. "Just the other day I saw him over here on his private time—it must of been, because he wasn't wearing his uniform—but he was talkin' to those drug boys. In broad daylight. You can't tell me somethin' isn't goin' on with that. You scared to even trust the police 'cause half of 'em are in on all this mess." Several people agreed.

"Make no mistake," McDougal stated, "there are some bad cops out there. If you have some information please give it to us and we'll have our Special Investigations Unit look into it." Francis noted silently that he wasn't going to give any information to anybody, and end up dead in an alley.

McDougal continued, "but one thing that I really want to stress in this meeting is that we need the help of the community. The police can't be everywhere at once, and the only way we can start to solve these problems is if the law-abiding citizens help us. We need your help. If you have information, please let us know about it. Maybe you see certain cars constantly stopping at a particular house. Well, you can write down the tag number, the date, the time—pass that information on to our Vice Unit. The more information we have, the better the evidence we can get to lock these guys up."

A man in the back of the room, Dennis Pettibone, stood and pointed at McDougal angrily. "I can't believe you're comin' in here and tellin' us to snitch on our own people. People in the community should refuse to get involved with cops. If you-all were serious about stopping this drug problem, you could do it. Black people don't own the planes that bring the drugs *into* this country. Black people don't own the gun shops in Virginia where all these weapons are coming from. My personal opinion is that this society *wants* black people out here sellin' drugs and killin' each other over a piece of rock. —And if we don't kill each other off, then the police are right there to do it for us. You askin' us to help you lock up more black men, more young black men? No, I don't think so."

Another resident entered the fray. "Now wait a minute Denny, I can understand what you're sayin' about the police brutality and all, but one thing you're forgetting is that these black people are out here killing other black people." The observation was correct: 93 percent of black victims were killed by other black people; the rate for whites killing other whites was 86 percent.

"I agree with you that if all this drug abuse and murder was happening to whites then they would have solved it yesterday."

"You got that right," said Pettibone.

"It's just like with the AIDS thing: as long as it was only killing off gay people and people in Africa and poor blacks and Puerto Ricans here, nobody cared. But now that you got these celebrities and other famous people dying, all of a sudden everybody's got all this sympathy for AIDS people.

"But I *do* want all this foolishness in the community to stop, and I'm willing to get involved. But the only thing is I don't want to give any evidence no matter *what* I see, because I'm scared of retaliation."

Getting tangible evidence and witnesses was a major problem in the prosecution of drug trafficking and other crimes. A review of the cases dismissed after an initial decision to prosecute showed that an exceedingly high proportion were dropped because of evidence or witness problems. (See Exhibits 13 and 14.) For example, in 1974 only 1% of victimless crimes including drug trafficking were dismissed for evidence problems, and 2% for witness problems. By 1990 26% of victimless crimes were being dismissed for evidence-related reasons, and 24% for witness-related reasons. These trends held for robbery and other violent crimes.

McDougal conceded, however, that there was good reason for citizens to be wary of testifying in drug cases. The intimidation and murder of

Exhibit 13:

CASES DISMISSED DUE TO EVIDENCE PROBLEMS*

Type of Crime	1974	1990
Robbery	2%	19%
Other Violent (Homicide, Rape, Assault)	1%	36%
Victimless (Drugs, Gambling, Sex Offenses	1%	26%

* Cases dismissed after initial acceptance by prosecutor.

Exhibit 14:

CASES DISMISSED DUE TO WITNESS PROBLEMS*

Type of Crime	1974	1990
Robbery	20%	43%
Other Violent (Homicide, Rape, Assault)	33%	58%
Victimless (Drugs, Gambling, Sex Offenses	2%	24%

* Cases dismissed after initial acceptance by prosecutor.

witnesses was now common. "I can understand how the people in this neighborhood would be afraid to come forward with information," he told those at the meeting. "I don't know exactly how to fix the problem but I know there has got to be some remedy available."

A woman in the front row spoke up. "You know, it's not just in these drug cases that people don't think the police do any good, or can protect you. The woman who used to live next door to me was beaten for years by her husband. The police would come but they wouldn't do anything—just tell him to go out and cool off or stupid things like that. She couldn't get a restraining order or anything. She eventually had to move because the man would not stay away. Lord, I remember that man would beat her something terrible and the police wouldn't do anything about it. I mean, you may not know how to protect people against drug dealers, but you should be able to protect a woman against somebody right in her own home who is trying to hurt her or kill her."

"You're right ma'am, the laws used to be really inadequate. But now we have special procedures for domestic violence cases. We don't even necessarily have to have the woman herself sign a complaint against him. If the officer sees that the woman is bruised, and the house is all torn up— he can make the arrest based on his own judgment."

Although their meeting with Captain McDougal did not satisfy Lydia Davis and her neighbors completely, some good did result from it. They got to know one of the officers on a personal basis and were willing to provide information on suspicious vehicles and other goings-on in the neighborhood. This led to several busts and the closing of three crack houses. Once residents saw that there would be confidentiality and visible results they were even more willing to work with the police. They began talking seriously about starting a neighborhood patrol group.

Burnett and Silver felt they had learned a great deal at the meeting, and were anxious to have other Task Force members hear some of the arguments that had been made. They asked Lydia Davis and some of her neighbors if they would attend the public hearings once they got underway. They were eager to do so.

"It's about time the Mayor started paying attention," said Martha Heywood. "It's just too bad they always wait for something bad to happen."

Summaries of Conclusions
Recent Studies

UNDERSTANDING AND PREVENTING VIOLENCE

Albert J. Reiss, Jr.

Those of you who have read the three panel reports to be presented this morning know that each includes many specific recommendations. Rather than report the recommendations of our Panel on the Understanding and Control of Violent Behavior, I shall begin by telling you about the panel's overall approach to the problem of understanding, controlling, and preventing violence and then point to some of our recommendations that I think might contribute to our discussions today.

Perhaps the first thing worth noting is that the panel concluded that it could not cover all violent harms; it chose to focus on interpersonal violent behaviors, especially those that are constructed as crimes. It therefore did not deal with the causes and consequences of violence considered by previous national commissions. Nor did it deal with suicide or other forms of self-harming by violent means.

The second thing worth noting is that we did not talk generally of violent crimes or violent behaviors. Rather, just as one doesn't spend a great deal of time talking about disease, but rather of a specific disease— even of a specific type of cancer—if one is seeking to prevent or treat it, we recognized the importance of trying to understand what leads to specific types of crimes that involve violent behavior or threats of violence, such as armed robbery or spouse assault or the different types of homicide, each with its own causes and means of prevention. Indeed, although it is important to try and understand what causes different types of violent behaviors and their consequences, an understanding of causes is not essential either to preventing their occurrence or to meliorating their consequences. We can determine what places a given population at risk as a prerequisite to prevention and control and how different interventions meliorate the consequences of violence.

The third thing that guided our deliberations was a recognition of the fragmented state of knowledge and understanding about violent behaviors because the scientific community fragments itself into disciplines, each pro-

Albert J. Reiss, Jr., served as chair of the Panel on the Understanding and Control of Violent Behavior, which produced the report summarized here (Albert J. Reiss, Jr., and Jeffrey A. Roth, editors; Washington, D.C.: National Academy Press, 1993). The generous assistance of Jeffrey A. Roth, staff director for the panel, is gratefully acknowledged.

viding only limited understanding. Some focus on the physiology and neurobiology of aggression or violence; others focus on individual propensities or psychological dispositions to violence; still others try to understand why some communities are more violent than others. We recommended that a reasonable policy for funding research on understanding violent behaviors would give priority to research proposals that involved at least two of these levels—for example, studying both community and individual factors to determine the relative contribution of each to given violent behaviors.

The fourth thing that guided our final deliberations was that we could find relatively few examples in which research or evaluation provided sufficient evidence to conclude that a particular violence prevention or reduction program should be recommended for implementation. In fact, we concluded that only a relatively small number were particularly promising enough to warrant continuing implementation and testing. There are reasons that is so, and among them is the fact that most evaluations are not planned as part of the introduction of a program to prevent violence or reduce its consequences. In other cases the evaluation design was too weak to reach a conclusion as to the program's effects on a type of violent behavior. A good example is community policing. Many police departments introduce what they regard as community policing, but few provide for evaluating its effectiveness. Accordingly, we recommended partnerships between the research community and the agencies that plan and implement violence prevention or reduction programs and that the evaluation should be designed and ready for implementation before an intervention begins. Continuing evaluation of a particular type of intervention can teach us what may be working and what to change.

The panel's report offers a blueprint for preventing and controlling violence while building knowledge about its causes. All of you are familiar with the statistical portrait of violence in America, so I shall not repeat those facts. Rather, I shall now draw on only a few of the panel's conclusions and recommendations that may be germane to our discussion here.

To begin, it is commonly assumed that punishment strategies are a deterrent. So why not just build more prisons and send persons who commit a violent crime to prison with longer sentences? That experiment has been tried, and research for the panel led to the conclusion that it is a very limited strategy for preventing violent behavior. While average prison time per violent crime nearly tripled between 1975 and 1989, about 2.9 million serious violent crimes occurred in 1989—almost exactly the same as in 1975. Longer sentences no doubt prevented some violent crimes. But if it prevented many, they must have been replaced by others.

Jails and prisons aren't useless *responses* after violence occurs, but experience with sentencing persons who commit violent acts shows they aren't enough. To substantially reduce violence in America, it must be *prevented* before it happens, by fixing what causes it or by reducing the risks of its occurrence. When we cannot prevent a violent act, we can determine how best to intervene so that its consequences are less harmful to victims, their families, and their communities.

Prevention may seem overwhelming because there are many different causes and types of violent behaviors—in communities where violence happens, in early childhood development, in neurological processes that underlie violent acts, and in situations that present hazards for violence. That very complexity, however, presents opportunities because every cause and every risk factor suggest a promising point for prevention.

We can reduce violence the same way medical scientists extend life expectancy—by attacking one type of disease or one cause of death at a time. We should abandon the traditional focus on preventing crime and violence and focus rather on the most promising ways that we can prevent different types of violence—just as we focus on preventing different types of disease. Just as there are many different types of cancer that have different preventive strategies, there are many different types of homicide and hence no single way to prevent homicide. The causes and means of preventing domestic violence are not identical with those for assaults in bars, just as the causes of skin cancer (exposure to ultraviolent rays) are not the same as the causes of lung cancer (smoking).

At the community level, "reducing poverty" is too general to serve as a launching point for violence prevention or reducing its consequences. Yet research suggests some promising and achievable objectives: reversing housing policies that geographically concentrate poor, one-parent families with teenage sons; supporting social networks and parenting whose values discourage violence; improving police-community cooperation; and providing legitimate economic alternatives to violent illegal drug and gun markets.

During childhood development, promising points of intervention and prevention include helping parents to be nonviolent role models, provide consistent discipline, limit children's violent entertainment, and teach them nonviolent ways to meet their needs. Regular postpartum home visits by public health nurses and, later, Head Start preschool enrichment, seem to help. Restricting the availability of *violent* sexual pornography may help reduce sexual violence.

The panel's report provoked concern over intrusions into the lives of minorities, epileptics, the mentally disabled, or children "marked" by some genetic pattern by simply opening the possibility of investigating neurological processes in causing violence. The panel found no scientific support for such intrusions, but concluded that reducing women's substance abuse during pregnancy, children's exposure to lead, and childhood head injuries would prevent some violence.

At best, these are long-range approaches to preventing violence. Faster results require eliminating hazardous situations for violence. That strategy points to three major commodities linked to aggression and violent behaviors: alcohol, illegal drugs, and guns. It also points to intervention into places and situations in which these commodities are more likely to precipitate violent behavior.

To prevent alcohol-related violence, police and proprietors can cooperate to diagnose and remove the risks in "hot spots"—places, including bars, that produce far more than their share of violence-related police calls. Some alcohol abuse prevention programs are promising. Laws, alcohol taxes, and social pressure to cut underage drinking have reduced teenagers' automobile accident rates and may reduce their excessive share of interpersonal violence.

Unlike alcohol, illegal drugs produce violence primarily through distribution, not use. Strategies to reduce drug demand that fuels violent markets include drug abuse prevention, drug treatment, and coordination of in-prison therapeutic communities with postrelease treatment. Methadone equivalents for cocaine and other drugs that could make drug treatment more effective show promising development.

Debates about firearm violence usually center on new laws, some of which have reduced gun murders temporarily. But because most guns used in crime are obtained illegally, the panel stressed finding better ways to enforce existing gun laws—especially disrupting illegal gun markets and preventing juveniles from buying guns. Such police tactics as undercover buys and wholesale-level sting operations may be useful. But as we should have learned from the "drug wars," making them work requires community support, evaluation, and progressive development.

Moving from promising points for intervention to effective violence prevention will require cooperation by organizations that don't always work well together: police; other criminal justice agencies; community-based organizations; school, public health, and social service administrators; and evaluation researchers. Ties among them must develop locally and around specific prevention efforts, but the federal government can encourage that development.

Finally, the panel concluded that federal antiviolence assistance should be reoriented to increase incentives for interagency cooperation and for long-term development and testing programs. Federal investments in research to understand violence will continue to pay off with new understanding of means for preventing it.

UNDERSTANDING CHILD ABUSE AND NEGLECT

Cathy Spatz Widom

Thank you. It's a pleasure to be here.

You may say to yourself, "I wonder why we have to hear about this report on understanding child abuse and neglect, given that the focus of this conference is urban violence?" Well, one thing is that child abuse *is* a form of family violence. So we should be concerned about that in itself. But what I will say in the few minutes I have is designed to tell you why understanding and preventing child abuse and neglect is important for urban violence, particularly so that we may be able to reduce urban violence in the future.

I was particularly excited and encouraged when I was at a community policing meeting several weeks ago and the keynote luncheon speaker was Attorney General Janet Reno. It was as if she had been in my brain the week before as I was making notes for my talk to those same community policing people about why and what they should do in cases of child abuse and neglect. And it's very exciting for me to hear an Attorney General of the United States talking about prevention, rather than simply law enforcement.

Al Reiss said at the start of his remarks that he was just going to just pick a fraction of things in his panel's report to tell you about. I have to say at the beginning, that in contrast to some other areas of knowledge that we have in the social sciences, the scientific study of child abuse and neglect is still in its early stages of development. And we desperately need more high-quality research to build a firm knowledge base.

The panel adopted an ecological, developmental perspective, which means that we wanted to look at the child in the context of the family and of society. This perspective reflects the understanding that development is a process involving transactions between a growing child and a social environment, and in that environment development takes place. The phenomenon of child abuse and neglect has moved from a theoretical framework, where we looked at individual disorders and pathology in parents, toward a focus on more extreme disturbances of child rearing—often part of a con-

Cathy Spatz Widom served as a member of the Panel on Child Abuse and Neglect, which produced the report summarized here (Anne C. Petersen and Rosemary Chalk, editors; Washington, D.C.: National Academy Press, 1993).

text of multiple family problems, such as substance abuse, mental illness, stress, or poverty. I'm not going to talk too much about theory, because I really want to focus on consequences.

Research in this field is beginning to demonstrate that the experiences of child abuse and neglect are a major component of child and adult mental and behavioral disorders. Research has suggested both a variety of short- and long-term consequences. Physical consequences range from minor injuries to severe brain damage and even death. Psychological consequences range from chronic low self-esteem to severe dissociative states and to higher rates of suicide attempts. The cognitive effects of abuse range from attentional problems and learning disorders to severe organic brain syndromes to low IQ and reading ability levels that persist very dramatically into young adulthood. Behaviorally, the consequences range from poor peer relationships all the way to extraordinarily violent behaviors. So the consequences of abuse and neglect not only affect the victims themselves, but also the larger society in which they live.

I want to talk to you and tell you about some of these consequences that are of a particular concern for our meeting here today and tomorrow. On the basis of some recent research that was funded originally by the National Institute of Justice, we found clear evidence that there is an increased risk of becoming a delinquent—that is, having an arrest as an adolescent—if one is abused or neglected as a child. The research was a prospective, longitudinal, cohorts-designed study with a large sample of abused and neglected children and a control group that was matched on the basis of age, race, sex, and approximate social class. Thus, the rates that I am reporting are independent of the characteristics of people that we already know are correlated with risk of arrest for delinquency.

This research showed a 53 percent increase of arrest for delinquency for abused and neglected children over the control children. Similarly, there was an increase in risk of arrest as an adult—38 percent over the matched controls. And there was also an increased risk in arrest for violent behavior of 38 percent. And, as you know violent *arrests* represent probably only the tip of the iceberg in terms of the kind of violent behavior that may be occurring in households and in neighborhoods. Abused and neglected children also get started committing crimes earlier, and they also are more likely to become chronic offenders.

So when we talk about violence I suggest, and our panel report suggests, that it's important to look at these abused and neglected children. And it's not just the physically abused children—although they do have the highest risk—but it's also the neglected children. Given that almost half of the officially reported cases of abuse and neglect in the United States are neglect, and that the smaller portions are physical abuse and sexual abuse, it seems very important to not ignore the cases of neglect, although they often are not as sensational as the cases of physical abuse and sexual abuse that receive so much attention.

Even for people who have low expectancies for getting into trouble— that is, girls in general have a much lower risk of being arrested—the effects of being abused are also very dramatic. We found a 77 percent increase for girls' having an arrest as a delinquent. One interesting finding is that this increased risk in juvenile violence is gender-specific for females; we don't see the same increase in juvenile violence for the abused males.

In this research there is also a puzzling race-specific effect, which we cannot explain, but which I would encourage everyone to think about more carefully. This effect suggests the need to be very sensitive in terms of the way we respond to abused and neglected children at the very earliest stages— so that when we first hear of a case of abuse and neglect, if we have services available *before* detaining children, we need to offer these services equally to black and white children.

Another thing that you have probably assumed, but for which we now have fairly good evidence, is that abused and neglected children are at increased risk of running away. And running away puts these already vulnerable children at further risk, since many of them report personal victimizations *after* they have run away.

I suggest to you that we need to be thinking about preventing child abuse and neglect before they happen. If we take the figure of an 11 percent arrest for violence through young adulthood and the figure of 1 million reports of child abuse and neglect per year in the United States, you can do the arithmetic to see the kind of violence bomb we are sitting on—if we do not do anything to prevent or intervene and provide services for these children.

In our report we have a chapter on prevention. I obviously can't talk about all the different prevention programs that have been attempted. Unfortunately, however, most of the prevention programs have not been evaluated, so that while there are many exciting and promising developments, we desperately need to have evaluations of these programs.

I do want to talk to you about one program that has been evaluated— although it's not a conclusive evaluation—and it seems to have some promise for the prevention of future maltreatment. This is a study by David Olds and his colleagues at the University of Rochester. It was originally done in Elmira, New York. The population is largely white and rural, so one might think that it does not have too much of a problem in terms of child abuse, but it was actually rated as having the highest reports of child abuse and neglect in New York State for approximately a 10-year period and also a very high rate of poverty. In that program, researchers systematically assessed the advantages, the effects, of using nurse home visitors, beginning with a pregnant mother. These women were environmentally at risk—that is, they were poor, single, young, and had a low education. They didn't necessarily all have those characteristics, but those were the eligibility criteria for this particular study. In some cases the researchers provided services prenatally, and in others both prenatally and postnatally; they provided parent education programs; and there were other efforts to enhance the family and to provide social support. They also—for those of you in transportation—included an element of providing transportation to medical facilities. What they found in this very elegant study (and, in fact, there was a control group) was that these home-visited families showed reduced risk in the number of child abuse and neglect reports in comparison with the control population. And the reduction was the most dramatic in the group of families who were at highest risk. Now this project is being replicated in Memphis, Tennessee, with a quite different population, and we all eagerly look forward to the results. But I suggest to you that in thinking about the prevention of child abuse and neglect and the possible spillover effects to violence, this might be a worthy inclusion in your plans.

There is also a program that is in effect in Hawaii now—it's called the Hawaii Healthy Start Program. It is intended to foster healthy development and family self-sufficiency. And it is largely on the model of these nurse home-visiting programs. In the future we hope to be able to report back and to say whether these types of interventions will be able to reduce further child abuse and neglect and, ultimately, violence.

One implication from these findings is that interventions with childhood victims of abuse and neglect need to occur early, so that they can have an impact on early stages of development. Given the demonstrated increased risk associated with this victimization, police, teachers, and health workers need to recognize the signs of abuse and neglect and take action and intervene early. Later interventions in adolescence should not be ignored, but the later the intervention in a child's life the more labor-intensive and the more difficult the change process become. Particular attention needs to be paid to abused and neglected children who have behavior problems, with indications of these problems occurring as early as 6, 7, 8, and 9 years old. These are the children who are most at risk for becoming chronic runaways. They are the children who are most at risk for becoming chronic offenders and violent offenders. And they are the children who account for the multiple placements in foster care and the revolving door placements that you see. In comparison with other abused and neglected children, these children with behavior problems have the highest rates of delinquency, criminality, and violent offending. It is not the case that foster care necessarily leads to problems with children, it may only be for a subset of these children.

I want to repeat and emphasize that increased attention needs to be paid to *neglected* children. Neglect is almost three times as common as physical abuse and sexual abuse cases, and yet the rates of arrest for violence are almost as high among these children as among the physically abused. We must not neglect neglect.

Finally, I'd like to encourage you to think more broadly about what you do to prevent future violence. There's a role for people in terms of community policing. We need to be creative. We need to get involved. You are the people who are making hundreds of crucial decisions each day about the lives and futures of these children. We are hopeful that we can design interventions to prevent future violence.

Thank you.

LOSING GENERATIONS:
ADOLESCENTS IN HIGH-RISK SETTINGS

Joel F. Handler

The concern of the Panel on High Risk Youth was the large and increasing numbers at-risk young people.

Most research concentrated largely on why individuals engage in high-risk behavior. As we worked, the enormous power of settings in shaping adolescent lives became apparent, It also became clear that the critical settings of adolescent life had deteriorated sharply over the last two decades. It was these settings that became the focus of our report.

Adolescents depend on families, neighborhoods, schools, and health systems. All of these institutions are now under severe stress. As the fault lines widen, more and more young people are falling into the cracks. Institutions and systems initially designed to help high-risk youth, such as juvenile justice and child welfare, have instead become sources of risk.

The social forces that are straining these institutions are many and complex, but they are all influenced by the relentless decline in income of families with young children. Family income is the single most important determinant of the settings in which children spend their formative years. Over the past two decades, the real incomes of young families have declined by almost one-third. Today, almost one-quarter of the families headed by a young adult have incomes below the poverty line.

Growing up in or near poverty exacts a heavy toll on children and adolescents. Adolescents from low-income families are more likely to have physical and mental health problems, to exhibit delinquent behavior, to show low academic achievement, and to drop out of school. They are less likely than their higher income contemporaries to get jobs. The numbers of poor adolescents who are unprepared for the world of adult work has grown alarmingly. Without a stable connection to the workforce, one remains outside mainstream society.

One-quarter of American children now live with only one parent, and poverty rates are almost six times higher for single-parent families than for two-parent families. Studies suggest that children of single parents are more likely to engage in such high-risk behavior such as drug and alcohol use and unprotected sex, to drop out of school, and to commit suicide.

Joel F. Handler served as chair of the Panel on High-Risk Youth, which produced the report summarized here (Washington, D.C.: National Academy Press, 1993).

Children born to adolescent mothers face the highest risk of failing to become successful adults.

Poor children are likely to grow up in socially disorganized, racially segregated neighborhoods, wit a high risk of becoming victims of drug-related violence, perpetrators of such violence, or both. These children are likely to go to schools that have fewer resources than those in more affluent neighborhoods. Although public schools have traditionally been viewed as the institutions through which poor children can rise above their socioeconomic roots, schools in poor neighborhoods have not in recent years been able to keep that promise. The many problems that poor students bring to the doorsteps have in most instances overwhelmed the resources and best efforts of the schools. And, unlike many industrialized countries, the United States does not provide an institutional bridge to help adolescents who are not college-bound make the transition from school to work.

The interplay of these conditions creates very different developmental opportunities for adolescents according to the income and race of their parents, the communities in which they live, and whether they live with one or both parents. Children born into poor families, living in high-risk neighborhoods, and attending poor schools know that their opportunities are limited, and significant numbers become alienated, lose hope, and fail to acquire the competencies necessary for adulthood.

How can we strengthen the institutions adolescents depend on and reduce the risks young people face?

Although it is quite true that these issues need more study, some of the problems are so acute and their effects so destructive that to delay action would needlessly endanger the future of more children. The report includes an agenda for further research and describes directions for change in the 1990s and beyond.

First, we must address the issue of supporting families. We must keep in mind that a rising economic tide will not necessarily lift most poor families out of poverty. Both the proportion and total of families living in poverty increased during the long period of economic expansion in the 1980s. Targeted intervention will be needed to enhance people's skills, provide entry-level job opportunities, and improve support services, such as child care. Income transfer programs will also need to be improved to assure families an adequate standard of living, safe housing, and access to essential services, such as health care. In designing these program and policy responses, care should be taken to encourage rather than punish the formation and maintenance of two-parent households.

Second, the crumbling infrastructure of inner-city neighborhoods must be dealt with. Affordable housing and safe recreational opportunities are urgently needed. Residential segregation must be addressed by all levels of government through incentive programs and the vigorous enforcement of fair housing laws and other civil rights laws and regulations.

Third, young people must have access to services that respond to the major threats to adolescent health—illicit drug use, cigarette and alcohol use, violence, teenage pregnancy, and emotional distress. But service programs will not be effective if they target just one particular high-risk behavior, such as drug use; they need to take a holistic approach to adolescents' life circumstances.

Although rigorous research of service programs is thin and often inconclusive, most experienced program practitioners agree on the importance of a sustained relationship with caring adults; opportunities for young people to succeed and rewards for those successes; opportunities to contribute and to feel in control; and opportunities to develop trust relationships.

Fourth, there is no integrated health or mental health system in the United States. Programs and treatments are built around specific pathologies. There is inadequate insurance and lack of preventive coverage. About one-third of parents cannot afford health insurance for themselves or their families. Overall, the system is uncoordinated and access is difficult for adolescents. The response to the major threats to adolescent health—substance abuse, violence, pregnancy, and emotional distress—is inadequate.

I am encouraged by the President's initiative in health care reform and what seems like a consensus on the need for universal coverage. However, for adolescents, insurance coverage, by itself, is not sufficient. Services must be available that emphasize disease prevention and health promotion. Moreover, these services must be consistent, comprehensive and coordinated, especially preventive services.

The single most important proximate threat to the lives of inner-city youth is the proliferation of firearms. The issue of guns requires urgent national attention. Measures to disarm this population must be explored.

Fifth, despite the wide and varied efforts at school reform and the increasing use of schools for preventive health services, sex education, and so forth, these reforms, for the most part, have not addressed the problems of inner-city youth. Only a few jurisdictions have addressed the politically explosive issue of inadequate school funding. School-based management and parental involvement cannot substitute for inadequate resources. There are serious questions about the impact of various choice proposals on the poorest schools in the worst neighborhoods.

Insufficient attention had been paid to the effects of instructional practices on the school performance of low-achieving schools. In fact, schools continue to use counterproductive interventions—such as rigid ability grouping (or tracking), grade retention, "pull-out" Chapter 1 programs, and categorical dropout prevention programs. Some schools and districts are experimenting with alternatives specifically focused on improving the achievement for at-risk children and youth—for example, heterogeneous and cooperative learning, the use of "bridging classes" rather than grade retention, and more academically oriented curricula.

We must remember that less than one-quarter of young people leaving high school will complete a 4-year college degree. There must be improved mechanisms to assist these people to prepare for and find entry-level jobs with a future. Research in other industrialized countries has found that the greatest successes are those programs that prepare young people for employment, but also include an explicit goal of facilitating overall youth development. What is needed are integrated and sequential academic instruction, occupational training, and work experience. The traditional approach—single-component programs usually of short duration—have few lasting effects.

Sixth, the report identified a number of ways in which the juvenile and criminal justice systems fail to intervene before adolescent offenders become fully enmeshed in the adult criminal justice system. We are all painfully familiar with the high proportions of inner-city youth, especially minorities, who have had official contact with the criminal justice system, and these contacts, in effect, mortgage an adolescent's future by jeopardizing long-term employment prospects. Particualr attention should be paid to ways in which the justice system seens to exacerbate racial, ethnic, and socioeconomic variations in life chances. We recognize that the criminal justice system is overwhelmed and is in need of considerable resources as well as reform. At the same time, we need to develop alternatives to conviction and incarceration.

Seventh, like the criminal justice system, the child welfare system is overwhelmed by rising caseloads. Adolescents seem to fare particularly poorly in the system—with mutiple placements and poor outcomes. There are conflicting pressures and controversies over the priority of family preservation and the need to strengthen families. But there is little research documenting the comparative effectiveness of alternative strategies, which severely limits policy and program initiatives.

In conclusion, one cannot emphasize too strongly the harmful effects of discrimination. A single act of discrimination—be it the denial of a job opportunity or the denial of housing in a sefe neighborhood—can have a powerful effect on an adolescent's life opportunities. Cumulativety, acts of discrimination create large socially and economically disenfranchised groups and blight the developmental opportunities of many American youths. Essential to the success of all efforts to improve the settings for adolescents is strong enforcement of laws against racial discrimination. Continuing efforts to abate discrimination must be made at all levels of society.

INNER-CITY LIFE: CONTRIBUTIONS TO VIOLENCE

Joan McCord

Joel Wallman of the Harry Frank Guggenheim Foundation deserves credit for bringing together the authors whose work will appear in "Inner-City Life: Contributions to Violence." In addition to editing the volume, I am writing the introductory and concluding chapters. The book draws attention to circumstances in urban America that contribute to contemporary violence and suggests means for its reduction.

"Inner-City Life: Contributions to Violence" begins with a chapter on historical and cross-cultural perspectives, setting violence in America into a larger framework. After this introduction, Eli Anderson takes a microscope to urban cultures that seem to breed violence. Rob Sampson then provides a multilevel examination of how communities, families, and individuals work through one another to diminish or increase violence.

Beginning with a chapter by Ron Slaby, who describes child development in inner cities, subsequent chapters focus on individuals. Terri Moffitt marshals evidences regarding neurological and psychological links to violence; Felton Earls and Jacqueline McGuire present a public health perspective on child abuse; and Nancy Guerra examines programs designed to reduce violence in urban America. The book ends with a summary that sets an agenda for improving life in inner cities through reduction of violence.

The common belief that U.S. cities have high crime rates is warranted. In fact, Al Reiss (1990) refers to crime rates in the United States as "outliers." What seems to be less widely known is that violence is not a new phenomenon in the United States.

Illegal violence has been evident through most of the history of the United States. Hollon (1974) identified 327 vigilante episodes responsible for 737 deaths between 1767 and 19190. Between 1834 and 1869, Boston, New York, Philadelphia, Cincinnati, St. Louis, Louisville, and Vicksburg were scenes of serious urban riots. Catholics, blacks, Irish, Mormons, and foreigners were among the targeted victims of mobs. Gurr (1989) reported more than 70 riots in New York City between 1788 and 1834, almost four-score riots by whites against freed slaves in the South within 10 years after the Civil War, 3,400 lynchings of black Americans between 1882 and 1951, and the violent history of labor organizing between 1870 and 1930.

Joan McCord is the editor of the book summarized here (New York: Harry Frank Guggenheim Foundation, 1994).

Throughout American history, protest movements turned to violence after civil attempts to achieve their goals had failed. Shays' Rebellion of 1786, an early sign of the agrarian movement aimed at changing laws to permit the use of paper money (Szatmary, 1980); the Whiskey Rebellion of 1794 expressing dissatisfaction with taxes imposed by a central government (Slaughter, 1986); anti-abolitionist riots of 1834 and the Draft riots of 1863 in New York City (Bernstein, 1990) are among the prominent early examples of politically motivated violence. Violent strikes form an important part of the American labor movement, with major strikes against the railroad in 1877 and a general strike in 1910 (Haller, 1973). In reviewing the historical pattern of violence in the United States, Brown (1989:26) noted: "Thus, given sanctification by the Revolution, Americans have never been loath to employ unremitting violence in the interest of any cause deemed a good one." The May 13, 1985, bombing of the house belonging to Move members in Philadelphia and the April 19, 1993, attack on Branch Davidians in Texas seem to confirm the point.

Blacks have been a part of American history since the early settlers arrived in Virginia. "The Negro helped to make America what is was and what it is," noted Quarles (1964:7), an historian trying to correct the silence about contributions blacks had made to what is right in America. When the Civil War began, there were 488,070 free blacks. In Chicago, where a small pocket of free blacks had formed a community, "the laws of the state forbade intermarriage and voting by Negroes. Segregation on common carriers and in the schools and theaters was widespread" (Drake and Cayton, 1945/1962:41). In Philadelphia between 1838 and 1860, while occupational opportunities for whites were increasing, "blacks were not only denied access to new jobs in the expanding factory system . . . they also lost their traditional prominence in many skilled and unskilled occupations" (Hershberg, 1973). Even after the Civil War, blacks were largely excluded from educational institutions and white collar occupations (Horton, 1993; Kirschenman and Neckerman, 1991; Lane, 1986; Steinberg, 1989; Thernstrom, 1973).

In counterpoint to this picture of inequality, American democracy sets out an ideal of equality. A presumption of equality underlies the belief that anyone can be successful. Being successful is, on this assumption, a sign of character and the proper basis for self-esteem and privilege.

Despite the importance of success, criteria marking success are difficult to discern in the United States. Small differences—a carpet, a larger desk, a name on the door—mark rank within organizations. These differences, however, are likely to have meaning only to a limited audience. Since subtle symbols of status are difficult to recognize in America, wealth and property therefore become the marks of status.

Coupled with the rhetoric of equality, the unequal distribution of goods represents injustice to many who are poor. This perception of widespread injustice tends to be confirmed through television—which shows wealth without labor, and violence often as justified.

This history of unequal opportunities and unequal benefits raise doubts about participating in a social contract. Yet such participation is necessary to avoid the Leviathan.

From his work on the streets of Philadelphia, Eli Anderson has gathered rich illustrations of the ways in which a street culture can adopt a code of violence. He talks about the importance of respect—by which he means respect in the local community.

Carrying oneself as though ready to fight may be a form of defence—or a signal to others to attack. The code of the street is also a code of exposure. In this culture, avoiding fights may result in dishonor.

The population of inner cities can be divided into two types of families. Decent families, who are ostensibly opposed to the values of the street code of violence, reluctantly encourage their children to learn it so they can negotiate in the city.

Other families fully embrace the code and actively socialize their children into it. The structure of the inner-city family, the socialization of its children, the social structure of the community, and its extreme poverty can be seen to facilitate the involvement of many maturing youths in the culture of the streets.

Many who live in inner cities believe in "the Plan." The Plan involves a genocide campaign against blacks. In order to protect themselves, some argue, blacks must take the law into their own hands.

Anderson suggests that to solve these problems, we must rebuild the social context of trust in the urban environment. We should reinvest in the cities, offering growth, development, education, and training.

Community structure is important mainly for its role in facilitating or inhibiting the creation of social capital among families and children. Concentration of poverty has multiplicative effects—bringing together blacks from single-parent families, the jobless, and the poor. With concentrated poverty, there are few socialized models to follow. Getting help from neighbors seems difficult.

High-risk areas are likely to increase probabilities for having babies who lack appropriate stimulation or who suffer neuropsychological impairment (from whatever source). Prenatal health problems, nutritional deficits, and exposure to toxins may increase risk for developing antisocial aggression leading to violence.

Programs designed to reduce antisocial behavior or to improve the wellbeing of those living in inner cities have not been well served in terms of evaluations. Preschool health-related home visits have gains that seem to be largely short term.

Not all preschool programs are effective, though High/Scope seems to have been so (Weikart and Schweihart, 1992). We need to learn what types of programs work.

Social skills training does not seem to be effective for inner-city children. In fact, there is some reason to suspect that when aggressive children are helped to become more socially skillful, the result may be increased aggression among their peers.

Secondary school prevention programs (e.g., attention control) have rarely received long-term evaluations. A comprehensive project in which children were given a range of services including daily feedback on school behavior and periodic parent-school meetings (Bry and George, 1980), according to Guerra, seemed to have benefits extending for 5 years.

Parent training appears to have some short-term gains, but low-income families are particularly difficult to reach. Recent evidence also suggests that parents who reject their own children and treat them inconsistently respond positively and consistently to other children, thus showing that they do not lack the skills for which they are being given training (Dumas and LaFreniere, in press). Guided group interaction appears to have had damaging effects (Gottfredson, 1987).

Nancy Guerra identifies two approaches as promising. One combines teaching about effects of gang participation with after-school athletic programs. Evaluations, however, have yet to confirm this impression of promise.

The other is a School Development Program, in which three teams have been created to address problems of the community by eliciting opinion from the community. These teams are designed to improve schools, to improve mental health, and to encourage paren participation (Comer, 1988). Again, unbiased information is awaited.

In sum, we desperately need good studies. Expert opinions should not continue to be the basis of choice for how to cure the nation's violence. Just as we protect society from innocuous and harmful medicines by first testing them and measuring their effects, we ought to be assessing our social programs for safety and potency before accepting them as effective. With properly designed studies, we can learn about the causes of violence by learning how to reduce it.

REFERENCES

Bernstein, I. (1990). *The New York City Draft Riots*. New York: Oxford University Press.

Brown, R.M. (1989). Historical Patterns of Violence. Pp. 23-61 in T.R. Gurr, ed., *Violence in America Volume 2: Protest, Rebellion, Reform*. Beverly Hills, Calif.: Sage Publications, Inc.

Bry, B.H., and F.E. George (1980). The preventive effects of early intervention on the attendance and grades of urban adolescents. *Professional Psychology* 11:252-260.

Comer, J. P. (1988). Educating poor minority children. *Scientific American*, 256:42-48.

Drake, S.C., and H.R. Cayton (1945/1962). *Black Metropolis: A Study of Negro Life in a Northern City.* New York: Harper & Row.

Dumas, J.E., and P.J. LaFreniere (in press). Relationships as context: supportive and coercive interactions in competent, aggressive, and anxious mother-child dyads. In J. McCord ed., *Coercion and Punishment in Long-term Perspectives.* New York: Cambridge University Press.

Gottfredson, G.D. (1987). Peer group interventions to reduce the risk of delinquent behavior: a selective review and a new evaluation. *Criminology* 25(3):671-714.

Gurr, T.R. (1989). *Violence in America Volume 2: Protest, Rebellion, Reform.* Beverly Hills, Calif.: Sage Publications, Inc.

Haller, M.H. (1973). Recurring themes. Pp. 277-290 in A.F. Davis and M.H. Haller, eds., *The Peoples of Philadelphia.* Philadelphia: Temple University Press.

Hershberg, T. (1973). Free blacks in antebellum Philadelphia. Pp. 111-134 in A.F. Davis and M.H. Haller, eds., *The Peoples of Philadelphia.* Philadelphia: Temple University Press.

Hollon, W.E. (1974). *Frontier Violence: Another Look.* New York: Oxford University Press.

Horton, J.O. (1993). *Free People of Color: Inside the African American Community.* Washington, D.C.: Smithsonian Institution Press.

Kirschenman, J., and K.M. Neckerman (1991). "We'd love to hire them, but . . .": the meaning of race for employers. Pp. 203-234 in C. Jencks and P.E. Peterson, eds., *The Urban Underclass.* Washington, D.C.: The Brookings Institution.

Lane, R. (1986). *Roots of Violence in Black Philadelphia 1860-1900.* Cambridge, Mass.: Harvard University Press.

Quarles, B. (1964). *The Negro in the Making of America.* New York: Collier Books.

Reiss, A.J., Jr., (1990). Perplexing questions in the understanding and control of violent behavior. *International Annals of Criminology* 28(1/2):23-29.

Slaughter, T.P. (1986). *The Whiskey Rebellion: Frontier Epilogue to the American Revolution.* New York: Oxford University Press.

Steinberg, S. (1989). *The Ethnic Myth: Race, Ethnicity, and Class in America.* Boston: Beacon Press.

Szatmary, D.P. (1980). *Shay's Rebellion.* Amherst, Mass.: The University of Massachusetts Press.

Thernstrom, S. (1973). *The Other Bostonians: Poverty and Progress in the American Metropolis, 1880-1970.* Cambridge, Mass.: Harvard University Press.